C000193249

**Theinspirational**series™
Overcoming adversity and thriving

# Stress in the City
## Playing My Way Out Of Depression

### BY ENOCH LI

We are proud to introduce The**inspirational**series™. Part of the Trigger family of innovative mental health books, The**inspirational**series™ tells the stories of the people who have battled and beaten mental health issues. For more information visit: www.triggerpublishing.com

## THE AUTHOR

Enoch Li was born and raised in Hong Kong and Australia. She has studied, worked or lived in the US, France, the UK, the Netherlands and China, and has travelled to more than 40 countries.

She worked as an international executive in a multinational corporation, however, she was forced to take time off work due to illness and depression. She spent her recovery cooking, practising Chinese calligraphy, reading and writing, and engaging in play – in short, learning to take care of herself and letting go of residual work stress.

Enoch Li is now a social entrepreneur. She founded BEARAPY to reduce burnout and mental health issues in workplaces and the community, through helping adults access their inner playfulness. Her unique approach blends the power of playfulness – creativity, stress management, and self-awareness – into her transformation and facilitation work. She holds a Master's degree in Law and studies Chinese calligraphy.

Enoch currently lives in Beijing and continues to fight the urge to be an overachieving perfectionist ...

First published in Great Britain 2018 by Trigger

Trigger is a trading style of Shaw Callaghan Ltd & Shaw Callaghan 23 USA, INC.

The Foundation Centre

Navigation House, 48 Millgate, Newark

Nottinghamshire NG24 4TS UK

www.triggerpublishing.com

Copyright © Enoch Li 2018

British Library Cataloguing in Publication Data

A CIP catalogue record for this book is available upon request
from the British Library

ISBN: 978-1-911246-97-8

This book is also available in the following e-Book formats:

MOBI: 978-1-912478-00-2
EPUB: 978-1-911246-98-5
PDF: 978-1-911246-99-2
AUDIO: 978-1-78956-046-6

Enoch Li has asserted her right under the Copyright,
Design and Patents Act 1988 to be identified as the author of this work

Cover design and typeset by Fusion Graphic Design Ltd

Printed and bound in Great Britain by Clays Ltd, Elcograf S.p.A

Paper from responsible sources

## www.triggerpublishing.com

*Thank you for purchasing this book.*
*You are making an incredible difference.*

Proceeds from all Trigger books go directly to
The Shaw Mind Foundation, a global charity that focuses
entirely on mental health. To find out more about
The Shaw Mind Foundation visit:
**www.shawmindfoundation.org**

## MISSION STATEMENT

*Our goal is to make help and support available for every*
*single person in society, from all walks of life.*
*We will never stop offering hope. These are our promises.*

Trigger and The Shaw Mind Foundation

Creating hope for children,
adults and families

# A NOTE FROM THE SERIES EDITOR

The Inspirational range from Trigger brings you genuine stories about our authors' experiences with mental health problems.

Some of the stories in our Inspirational range will move you to tears. Some will make you laugh. Some will make you feel angry, or surprised, or uplifted. Hopefully they will all change the way you see mental health problems.

These are stories we can all relate to and engage with; they are stories of people experiencing mental health difficulties and finding their own ways to overcome them with dignity, humour, perseverance and spirit.

Enoch's story gives us a fascinating insight into the detrimental mental effects of self-imposed high standards, over-working, societal pressure, work-related stress and burnout. Though Enoch talks about this personally within the context of her own Chinese upbringing – she frequently refers to her mother as a Tiger Mother and herself as a Tiger Cub – she also explores this phenomenon within the global community, and especially within corporate organisations. Her reflections on the importance of understanding, embracing and facing your emotions also offer the reader some helpful strategies with which to move forward.

This is a well-written, hard-hitting and unique approach to mental health, one that you may have never come across before.

This is our Inspirational range. These are our stories. We hope you enjoy them. And most of all, we hope that they will educate and inspire you. That's what this range is all about.

**Lauren Callaghan**

*For Timmie, Rivie, and Arlie, who remind me to be playful. For Floppie and the bears, for being the rationality in my irrationality.*

**Disclaimer:** Some names and identifying details have been changed to protect the privacy of individuals.

**Trigger Warning:** This book contains references to thoughts of suicide, suicide attempts, overdosing, hallucinations and self-harm.

# CONTENTS

*Depression is a blinding light. Amidst despair and defragmentation, I began to see myself. The haze before my eyes lifted.*

*Depression is an avalanche. Stuck under 50 feet of snow, I had no choice but to stay with myself, my discomfort, and introspection.*

*Depression is a protest. My body, mind, and heart had had enough of doing what I thought should be done.*

*Depression is a message. Something within me had to change. I wanted to "get out of it".*

*Depression is a mentor. A guide to finding the inner playfulness that I had lost in the process of growing up.*

*Play makes life bearable. Play is thinking. Play is a language. Play is self-awareness.*

*May adults learn to be playful again.*
*May kids never lose their ability to play.*
*And may parents not wean playfulness out of their children.*

*For a mentally healthy world.*

# PROLOGUE OF VANITY

I sank into my leather seat, kicked off my heels, and reached down to massage the soles of my feet. I had filled every single minute on my schedule for this business trip, and this first one saw me on a flight from Paris to Shanghai. I switched off my Blackberry and chucked it into my leather handbag, which I had bought in Florence on a weekend trip. The air steward returned with the newspapers I'd requested, along with a blanket. I stretched out under the duvet and discreetly pulled down the footrest with my feet, hoping that the steward would not catch me and make me stow it away during take-off. I wished I could snuggle up and catch some sleep during the flight – it was the one time I didn't have to bother checking my Blackberry for urgent office emails – but I exercised some self-control and began scanning the headlines. The commodities market seemed to be flourishing, and there was some news about a new type of fund. I didn't understand what it was about, and so made a mental note to myself to look it up after landing. Maybe it would prove useful for the Chartered Financial Analyst examination preparations.

I felt like a dignitary flying Business Class. Glancing around, I realised smugly that I must have been the only woman wearing a business suit in this cabin. At 25 years old, I must have been the youngest, too. I hoped that none of them could see through my relaxed façade and guess that I had no idea what I was doing, or that I could understand no more than one per cent of what was in the newspapers I was reading. The writing appeared to be in

English, but it made no more sense to me than a child's babbling all strung together. The market goes up and the market goes down. That was all I knew.

I hadn't anticipated a career in banking. I was attracted to working internationally, and less to the idea of numbers and excel spreadsheets. Once I started though, I enjoyed the experience and thought I could do it forever. And then, perhaps someday after I retired, I could go back to international criminal law and do some good for the world. I felt compelled to be distinguished from the day I was selected as one of only 20 students to enrol in the double bachelor's degree program in Law and Politics. Tertiary education usually takes a mere three years in Hong Kong – and young, naïve busybodies are transformed into suit-wearing executives, lawyers, accountants, and salespeople in the blink of an eye. Even after they are transformed they are probably just as naïve, except now they're doubly loud and arrogant simply because they have the backing of a degree on their CV — triply loud if they have graduated with First Honours.

I refused to be lumped into this immature category. I was convinced that this international executive job would set me apart from the amoebic thinking of my peers, whose life ambitions involved nothing more than saving money to buy a 30-square-metre apartment in downtown Hong Kong, and a car if they got a bonus.

I would start higher up and sprint to senior management. I would dive into the deep end of the pool for my own good, and move to a new city every two to three years. I would be groomed to be CEO. Most of all, I would have a permanent expatriate package.

After a month-long, multi-stage assessment for this international executive position at the bank, the softly spoken lady from Human Resources had called me in Hong Kong. I was just walking from my last law lecture of the year towards the library to start studying for my final examinations. I had to cover the speaker to muffle the sound of my weeping when she gave me the offer to join the bank. I clamped my dark blue Nokia flip phone closed and tried to control my hysterical sobbing. The emotion was so intense that I couldn't describe it. It wasn't just gratitude or ecstasy; it was a bit of both, a combination of vindication and relief that I was not part of the mediocrity.

My excitement fizzled into tears, for I was able to finally cast off my Hong Kong life. I felt as if a sudden weight had been lifted off my shoulders. I was exonerated, free to fly wherever I wanted, in whichever way I chose. I would be living on my own, having rid myself of the chains I had towed with me. My monotonous student life had culminated in glory, meaning that I wouldn't need to walk down the same path as everyone else. At last, I was beginning the glamourous life for which I had spent years grooming myself. The determined university student would metamorphose into a posh businesswoman who would live in Paris and take meetings in Geneva, London, Tokyo, and Shanghai. I would never, ever again fly Economy Class.

Now, back on my flight from Paris, we were fast approaching Shanghai Hongqiao airport and were expecting to land in 40 minutes. The cabin crew started to prepare for landing: footrest up, tables upright and secured, cups and last bits of rubbish collected. The curtains that separated the worthy in Business Class and the unfortunates in Economy were drawn, though I could glimpse into the commoners' area. I caught the eye of a young man who peered forward as I looked back. I imagined he was trying to get a glimpse of what the world of Business Class looked like.

This geeky young man reminded me of myself only two years ago, when I was traveling to Paris from Hong Kong for my undergraduate study exchange year. I had packed two full suitcases, and my luggage was immensely overweight. The ground staff would not make an allowance for me, so I had to repack then and there at the airport with my mother's help. I still remember the haughty look a staffer in a pompous red uniform gave me, as if I was an underling of the underprivileged world who did not deserve to have a favour bestowed upon me. *Woe betide him should I one day become powerful and mighty,* I thought. *He might have to lose face and allow me an extra 5kg onboard.*

Indeed, I travelled on a shoestring budget for the remainder of my student days. I scoured for student discounts, rationing a small portion of money each day for water, food, and an occasional steak baguette with fries when it got too cold outside. Never again was I to be humiliated in such a way!

Now I was obsessed with my frequent flyer status. My heart skipped a beat whenever the mileage counter went up and I qualified for Gold status. I would spend a whole week mourning if I had not flown enough that year and was demoted to Silver. I started toying with the idea of buying Business Class tickets even when I travelled on holiday. And why not? I worked hard; I deserved something comfortable, right?

Stretching out on my flat bed up in the air is but a reflex now. And waiting for my menu with the vast choices of gourmet dishes and fine wine carries no novelty. But I remember when one day, by chance, I walked into the cabin via first class. I wondered to myself then: *who gets to fly first class? How do I make enough money to do so, so I can roll around on a wider flat bed?* I eyed my mileage account like a hawk as the card changed to a more glorious colour each year. For me, it was the ultimate status symbol.

I looked at this young man peering over the seats at me on the airplane, and I passed verdict. I decided he was not of the calibre to ever make it to my world, however good-looking he might have been. Some people have the potential, some people don't. Some will simply be stuck in their mental castes forever.

I shrugged off his eye contact and turned back to my bit of paradise, which was populated with middle-aged executives. They were endowed with receding hair lines, balding grey pates, and protruding beer bellies, all of which evidenced dedication to their powerful jobs and responsibilities in their respective companies. I snapped back into consciousness when the air steward brought me back my long cashmere coat, which I carefully laid on my lap.

From the airport I travelled to the east side of the river that ran through the heart of Shanghai. Here my meetings for the next three days would take place. Pudong was the new central business district, and it housed banks, law firms, accountants, corpulent oil companies, and the headquarters of other international corporations. It reminded me of Canary Wharf in London: a dismal piece of wasteland that the government decided to carve out and transform into important buildings with floor-to-ceiling windows. Inside, corporate executives would sit in front of their computers every day and change the world for the better by stimulating the economy somehow. However glorious it looked on the outside, it still felt soulless.

I was empty inside too, but the glamour of power and a fat salary package, the lure of authority, and the illusion of importance hid all the pretence. They forged the mask I wore every day to fit in.

I could see beyond the Paris posting that I was currently in with the company. I was studying for the Chartered Financial Analyst exams and had started a master's in Law through University of London's distance learning program. I needed a backup plan in case the bank didn't work out for me, so I prepared for the Graduate Management Admission Test (GMAT) and business school applications for a few years down the line. These would bolster me in the banking sector and give me other opportunities to pursue. I pressed myself to achieve it all within a year, even if it meant I didn't have much time on the weekends to socialise.

I would slot in a weekend here and there to travel. I loved travelling alone – I savoured the liberty of staying at the museum until closing without having to consider anyone else, or eating as I pleased without needing to stay within a companion's budget. I hopped over to Budapest, Amsterdam and Florence in between exploring French coastal towns. But the weekend holidays did not rejuvenate me or alleviate the pressure I put on myself. They simply served the purpose of putting a check next to more and more cities on my list, just so I could say I had visited them. They just allowed me to have "well-travelled" as another badge of honour. I was blinded by society's standards and expectations – if I had a well-paid job, a big apartment, holiday breaks, and a social life, then I should be happy. Why would I not be?

Assuming that that's the definition of happiness, the irony was that I didn't have the energy to be happy. I had the spare time, but I was too bogged down by these images and reputations I had to create: the caring friend, the cool boss, the loving child, the efficient one. I spent all my energy living up to these standards – either those that others imposed on me or, even worse, those I *presumed* were imposed by others. I thought they would make me loved and liked. Consequently, my spirit and vigour started to erode. Some days, when I was supposed to be studying, I would just lie in bed until four o'clock in the afternoon, feeling lethargic. When I could push myself out of bed in the evening to make myself a pot noodle, I would berate myself for delaying the study plan and progress.

I had a life plan in the form of a Microsoft Word document that I followed to the letter, listing things I was to accomplish by the time I was 26 years old, by the time I was 30, 35, and so on. It was just all achievements or qualifications. It consisted of a list of cities I would like to visit, such as Buenos Aires and Rio de Janiero, and things to do before I died, like seeing the Northern Lights and polar bear cubs. I noted down activities I would like to do such as sky diving and parachuting, plus going to a fashion show. Planning was paramount. It gave me a direction and a sense of purpose, even though I had no idea where I was going and what my destination was – retirement? Retirement seemed a long way away for a young adult of 25. Pondering the meaning of life could wait; I had to sit through my Paris posting first.

During my Paris posting I became restless and wondered where I would end up next. I often felt awkward in social situations, standing around with a glass of wine in hand, moaning about work and the absurdity of French politics. But somehow, I pulled off a suave stature. I drummed away the rest of the posting, met my targets, found some friends, and enjoyed summer in Paris.

My relocation at the end of the Paris posting felt glamorous: a professional team of movers packed up my clothes and stuffed toys while I sat and watched them load my life into a cargo container. I laboured to uphold an image of a happy Enoch, basking in my high life, being young and free. I had no cause for complaints.

I was not even sure what I was feeling as I watched these two men wrap every little piece of the last 18 months in bubble wrap. They put each piece into boxes like toy blocks, compartmentalising them so that there was no dead space. I giggled a little when they had to lift the aubergine-coloured chaise longue I had bought at Galeries Lafayette through the window and down an extendable elevator from the back of a truck.

Two days later, I took my remaining possessions in two fat suitcases to Charles de Gaulle airport. I wiped away tears of relief as I boarded – I was elated to be leaving Paris again! Although Paris symbolised romance, style and fashion for most people, for me it was a soulless city of reclusion engraved into Renaissance style brick walls, ornamented with unfeeling statues. I had no return date, but I didn't think it would be any time soon. I sank into my flat bed and relished in the knowledge that I would have the time of my life during my next posting in Tokyo. I would also excel at my job. I even bought a whole new wardrobe of suits to match my new managerial position.

I was sure the air steward was flirting with me at one point and wanted to take me to dinner. Smiling politely, I declined. I snuggled up among the duvet blankets, stretched my legs, and entered my dream world for about eight hours before touchdown. It was comforting to know that, upon exit from customs, I would find someone holding up a placard with my name on it, and that they would then take me to a limousine and drive me around to inspect some of the best properties in Tokyo so that I could decide on my next home.

Another adventure was about to begin. My secret resolution for these coming few years was to focus solely and completely on work. I was going to earn myself the highest rating possible. Career was my life. Work was my life.

At least I was flying Business Class.

**Figure 1:** *Snobbie.*
*Snobbie is the guardian of the car, but occasionally gets out and about. He likes to people-watch, but he is exceptionally self-righteous and judgmental about what people wear and how they behave. He laments the lack of etiquette around him. He thinks he's cruising in a Porsche Cayenne but really it is just a normal SUV. He needs bringing back down to Earth.*

# THE OVERACHIEVER

"Oh, you can't help that," said the Cat: "We're all mad here.
I'm mad. You're mad."

Alice in Wonderland
Lewis Carroll[1]

# CHAPTER 1

# IMPOSTOR

When I was in Tokyo, I was the invincible superwoman who had it all. Yet unbeknown to me, the corrosion had already started.

No woman wants to be considered weak or pathetic, or to risk the career they have been slaving away towards for years. Often, we maintain the image of strength. There are many people of my generation who, like me, are ambitious and addicted to the perks that go along with high-flying corporate jobs. We have no time to pause and evaluate our health or our happiness – after all, who wouldn't be happy traveling the world, making an impressive salary, and accumulating accolades and praise for a job well done?

This stands doubly true for female executives hammering through the glass ceiling. We jet-set in our stiletto heels, attending business meetings across time zones and relishing the view from our hotels, offices and airports. We are far less likely to admit to depression – even if we allowed ourselves to suspect we might be stressed or burnt out. How could we be expected to share our inner turmoil, when to be seen as anything less than capable and adaptable could mean the end of our bright career trajectories, and our paths to conventional happiness? We should be happy and cheerful all the time, even when we're not.

Like every strong woman, my main priority at work was to out-perform and over-deliver. My second priority was to be cool, calm, and collected. I was to never let anyone guess I was angry or annoyed. I was to be patient with everyone. Polite but firm. Assertive but not bitchy. Outspoken but not loud. Sociable but not promiscuous. This was the image I wanted to promote, for I knew the corporate world was not kind to women, and the banking arena belonged to men. I had to win people over by not succumbing to the stereotypes of a weak, diffident or overly autocratic female manager.

Every morning, I took the Ginza line from Omotesandō Station to the office. The 25-minute train ride was spent scrolling through my Blackberry to filter out the emails that needed attention in the office. I would type a quick reply to a few easy ones as the train jolted between stations. News was slotted into a specific folder to go through over a cup of coffee towards mid-morning. By the end of the journey, I would have in my head a visual plan of the amount and priority of work that awaited me. On the off-chance that I had a few minutes left, I would pretend to be disinterested and stare into space ahead of me, while actually taking the opportunity to survey the sleeping Japanese salarymen sardined between one another. I often wondered if any of them actually relished their lives.

In preparation for my move to Tokyo, I had read up on business etiquette and culture to ease my immersion into the land of the rising sun. As a result, I was nervous and jittery. A banking world overflowing with testosterone – coupled with a culture that preferred men and seniority in age – meant double scoops of challenge for me. Being female and at least half the age of every other executive was not something I could change. I had to convince them with my abilities and results. To me, success did not just mean I was effective as a manager or efficient in my work; it also meant I had to be well-liked. Reputation was key. A mentor once cautioned me that it took years to establish a reputation, but only seconds to destroy it. I chanted this like a religious mantra and kept my opinions to myself, maintaining the serene image I had crafted.

Frustration and anger would boil up inside me when colleagues from other departments were not helpful or did not pay me due deference. The traders would ignore my calls and the sales team would never have time to meet my clients. I swallowed it all and flushed it down the toilet bowl during my mini-escapades to placate myself. It was not until I referred a massive deal to one of them that anyone started to take notice of my name or answer one out of the five phone calls I made to them.

The parade of men eyed me with suspicion. To them, I must have been a child in oversized skirts and heels trying to look like an adult. I felt belittled, but I was patient and kept my cool during meetings. A few times, when my sensible voice was ignored, I excused myself to go to the ladies so I could cry, vent my frustrations, sit for a few minutes to let the red in my eyes fade and then go back into the meeting room as if nothing had happened. Then I would repeat myself with more conviction until one of the gentlemen agreed with me and vouched for my opinion. Passive aggression was easier to weather than the outright harassment faced by some of the other female executives, so I did not protest. Over time, I gained their trust and respect by proving my worth with my performance. And it wore me out.

The only immediate outlet I had during work hours was Japanese class. I wanted to practise the Japanese I had learnt and, in half-broken Japanese and half-English, I would recount the week with my teacher. I seemed to click well with my language teachers, perhaps because I was not competing with them in any way. My Japanese instructor became a sounding board to whom I could vent. I would disclose my innermost thoughts: what my managers were like, what the team was like, and what crap I was dealing with. I would tell her who I liked and who I did not like. We became good friends and I trusted her discretion.

Unfortunately, I eventually had to cancel my classes as work took up more and more of my time, and I couldn't afford to be away from my desk if I wanted to leave the office at decent hours – especially with the onset of the financial crisis in 2007 and throughout 2008.

The setback was systemic. Companies across industries had to cut costs and lay off employees to keep the businesses afloat. I worked doubly hard and managed to make money to meet my targets. My bosses were supportive and gave me responsibilities to stretch me. People saw perseverance in my pale complexion. Once, my assistant whispered in my ear, 'Maybe you should put on some make-up before heading to see the client; you look tired.' I waved her off but relented after seeing my reflection in the mirror and dabbed some blusher on my cheeks. While everyone was holding onto their jobs like lifelines, I thrived for another year and came out with top ratings. My boss told me to take time off to rest, but I denied my fatigue, even after seeing my results from a compulsory online psychological wellbeing test they gave me.

At that point, the results of an employee wellbeing survey I had taken a year ago at the Tokyo office flashed into my memory:

"Enoch, you are extremely stressed, and we suggest that you see a counsellor."

The company took care of its employees' wellbeing as best as it could, and I had been offered two sessions for free in Tokyo after the survey results. I had confided in my boss, and he agreed I should go see the counsellor, especially as it was all confidential. So I did.

My first experience with a counsellor made me dismiss the profession because I thought I knew better. Plus, she gave me no tangible solutions. Being my arrogant self, I kept competing with the counsellor to see how much more I knew about psychology than she did. She listened, nodding at my complaints about my frequent colds, my desire to be promoted, and occasional frustrations at unhelpful colleagues – but she didn't say much. That was as far as it all went.

As we say in Chinese, "the ice does not stand at three feet only in one day's cold." Stress accumulated slowly, stealthily, and silently. I did not recognise the signs – and even if I had, I would have dismissed them. I tricked myself into believing that, as long as I frequented spas to sleep and rest, swam regularly, and had a social life, I would be free from any work-related or ersonal tension. I was lonely and overwhelmed but refused to admit it. I did not know that my body was at its limits; I thought I was flexing my muscles and pushing past my comfort zones.

The fundamental issue, both in my case and in so many others, is that hardly anyone talks about stress or depression, especially not people in the position I was. Depressed or not, work-related stress is not the best subject to discuss with clients over dinner, nor does it make for the best gossip with colleagues over coffee. In such a culture, is it any wonder that sufferers of depression keep their afflictions cloaked in cheerful-yet-determined professionalism? There is no place for discussions of stress-induced depression in the corporate world. It is professionally dangerous.

There are numerous causes of depression, including biological conditions. But one of the major causes is the leading source of stress in most people's lives: pressure at work. In a survey of 800,000 workers across more than 300 companies conducted by the American Institute of Stress, the number of employees calling in sick because of stress tripled from 1996 to 2000, and the numbers continue to rise[2] almost two decades later. In the same report, The European Agency for Safety and Health at Work reported that over half of the 550 million working days lost annually in the US from absenteeism are stress-related, and that one in five of all last-minute no-shows are due to job stress.

Here in China, the statistics are staggering in terms of how much time and money is lost as a result of depression or related illnesses. In its 2017 report, the WHO estimated that, in China, the total years lived with disability due to depressive disorders is 8,981,401[3]. "Years lived with disability" is used to measure the burden of disease and is calculated by how many years the illness causes disability, multiplied by the duration of the disability[4]. The concept of the global burden of disease was first introduced in 1996 and is used to quantify the burden of premature deaths and disabilities caused by major diseases in the world[5]. Each disease is allotted a weighting to reflect its severity, with 0 being perfect health and 1 being death[6]. In addition to being the leading cause of disability worldwide (according to the WHO[7]), depression's weighting of 0.76[8] means that it is a major contributing factor to the global burden of disease.

Even if we cannot grasp the statistical concept, eight million years is an enormous amount of time spent in disability – too much, if you ask me. But I didn't give it a second' thought until I became aware that I was contributing to that number myself.

One very late night in Tokyo I rubbed my eyes, stretched and felt the now-familiar soreness in my lower back. I hadn't even noticed that it was two o'clock in the morning, which was, in all fairness, much later than the typical night in the Tokyo office. However, I wasn't tired in spirit. I was rather motivated at having been entrusted with an important task assigned to me by my superiors – so motivated that I thought the task worthy of neglecting my lower back pain. It was a stubborn knot caused by sitting too much and carrying heavy files in my handbags as I trudged to client meetings in my heels. It had started back in Paris, where I would have to pay an exorbitant amount for a masseuse to soothe out the muscles.

The green digits twinkled on the screen and my vision blurred. *That's enough for one night,* I thought.

I was exhausted, having slept only five hours a day in the past week. But, in some idiosyncratic way, I felt fulfilled for having finished the tasks before me.

Work was on track, and my social life prospered in Tokyo. Life finally felt comfortable. When I moved to Tokyo from Paris, I was determined to have the time of my life and enjoy it instead of indulging in books each weekend. There was no shortage of people around me. There were bankers, artists, lawyers, teachers, head hunters, television celebrities, models, and executives ... The effervescence of the crowd and my friends made my head spin. People kept coming and people kept going – I couldn't keep up! And in the midst of the whirl of colour that was my social life, there was within me a melancholy that was more marked, a profound annihilation. Something was missing.

I was a hamster running non-stop on a wheel in a small cage. However bright a lime green or magenta it was, it was still a cage. A claustrophobic one at that. The glass doors boxing me in provided an illusory sense of comfort and contentment. It was the world in which I was brought up and told to follow the rules, to abstain from drink and drugs. It was the world in which I was told not to have sex before marriage because it was unholy, and to attend Sunday school every week. It was suffocating.

I gazed out to the unknown world, wondering if there could be life beyond the constricting walls of the cage.

No one seemed to understand why I was dissatisfied with my current environment. To every other hamster, it seemed that I had the best layer of hay under my little paws. I was in my prime, and the future could only be dazzling with a pristine career path, luxury apartments, captivating parties, and important business trips.

I did not want to be a hamster. Every time I ventured towards the cage door, I could hear my mother growling and feel her disapproving eyes boring into my back. I would open the door for a peek and slump back in anguish.

I should have enjoyed what I had! I should have learnt to be grateful! Surely I should have been happy in my company role – it was what was expected of me after gaining top honours in university!

Was it wrong to want something different? Was it rebellious to want to explore? I imagine anyone who peered into my life would criticise me for being an ungrateful little prick; there were starving children in Africa, and even homeless people just next door – I should have been thankful I had a job! I pacified my conscience by helping to distribute food to the homeless at Ueno Park every other Sunday afternoon.

The little voice in me warned me to take time to breathe. It jumped up and down to catch my attention. Life didn't need to be this way – not the way I was living it. I didn't need to eat instant noodles every day. I didn't need the obsession with the title on my business card. My body conspired against me, giving me frequent colds and drowning me in chronic fatigue. I swatted it away as though with a tennis racket. Oppressed by peer pressure and obsessed with what society considered success – money, a title, a corporate job – I soldiered on.

Like most others of my generation, I was fast paced and would become annoyed and impatient if instant gratification was two seconds late. I wanted to show everyone I could succeed as a woman, as a young person. I was there to defy all odds. I was energetic and demanded flexibility, looking for more than just a job to put bread on the table. My career path had to be clear and give me opportunities for personal development and training, not to mention provide me with business travel so I could stay at top hotels around the world, even if I had no time in between meetings to soak in the pools. The company had to keep me interested so I could chase my dreams through the platform of bureaucracy sooner rather than later. I wanted to set up my corner office with floor-to-ceiling glass windows. I was convinced I was invincible.

I couldn't haul reality up to my standards and expectations. But I would persevere at all costs, even to the detriment of my health and my relationship.

Timmie and I had a massive argument once in the middle of the night. I fell asleep after tossing and turning for two hours in bed. At 3.29am, I woke up – as had become habitual for me in the wake of the financial crash. I rubbed my eyes, sat on my pillow, and turned on my Blackberry, which I had hidden under the bed to prevent me from checking it in the middle of the night. The green light turned into a red blink: 20 new emails had come in from the European and American offices. I started to reply, my newly manicured nails tap-dancing across the keys.

Timmie was displeased to say the least. I had jostled him and he had woken up. Since moving from his matchbox apartment into my spacious one in Tokyo, he had become fed up with his sleep being continuously disrupted every night. He shot up from beneath the blankets, snatched my beloved electronic device from my hands and hurled it into the sliding door that separated our bedroom from the living room. The little black machine rebounded on the door into the wall and landed next to my beanbag. It continued to beckon me, its red light blinking at two-second intervals in accordance with the Circadian rhythm. I was horrified – that phone was my lifeline! I scrambled out of bed, but Timmie held onto my hand. He threatened to move out if I proceeded to rescue my Blackberry and read any more emails in the middle of the night.

I was ambivalent. I knew he had reason on his side, but my overseas colleagues were standing by for my reply – I did not lack in my delusions of grandeur and importance. I was agitated and contemplated my next course of action. Timmie mistook my moment of silence as surrender. He picked up my Blackberry before I could react and put it face down outside near the door. I glanced at the clock next to my bed. It said 4.05am. I consoled myself with the knowledge that I could get to the emails in two hours and reluctantly pulled the pillow over my head in an attempt to go back to sleep. I lay there for another hour and dozed off as the sun peeped through the curtains.

The next morning I made a pact with Timmie: once I got home I would turn the Blackberry off and hide it in my handbag until the next day. I kept my end of the bargain about 40 per cent of the time; I'll admit to sneaking into the bathroom when he was not looking to have a quick scroll through my emails! It was an addiction – one I knew I had, but still allowed to devour me.

Paradoxically, my disinterest in the corporate world grew like a tumour even as I persevered with my business school applications and toyed with quitting my job without an exit plan. I felt lost and confused, not knowing what I really wanted. What was the point of another promotion? I wished I could be in school again, where life was straightforward: achieve, accomplish, and achieve more. Now I could decide what to do with my weekends and spare time, and yet I didn't know what I wanted to do or where to go.

I used to dream of days with free time in which to read every novel I could get my hands on, yet the books I bought each time I passed through an airport remained untouched on my bookshelves. I would start on page one but fail to keep my eyelids open. I thought having a job meant financial security and the freedom to use my time without curfews or debate competitions on the weekends. I thought I could sit in the café under the trees to write poems, to compensate for lost time studying physics or calculus. I tried to force myself to write more again and scribbled down ideas for writing a book. I had wanted to publish a book since I knew books existed, but most thought being an author would not pay the bills. I missed the days when I could let my sentiments flow in waves of words, but my mind would go blank and I could only flip my pen in between my fingers and doodle.

I was exhausted, and even mint chocolate-chip ice cream could not lift my spirits.

I was in the office by half past seven every morning to read that day's newspaper headlines and mull over the internal systems I had to learn for my job. By nine o'clock the rest of the office would have rolled in with quiet order, and my boss and I would set about our meetings for the day. I had an average of four client meetings in one day during the first few weeks, with Japanese classes sandwiched during lunch. Occasionally I would miss lunch because I was too engrossed in my work. I would make up for it with a snack and a coffee in the afternoon. It made me feel faint at times, but I persisted through the day.

After my last meeting I would drag my weary soul back to the office at six o'clock in the evening to type up call reports, minutes, and other proposals. I reasoned with myself that I could work more efficiently in a limousine-like taxi than in the subway, so I would hop into a silvery black Benz idling just outside Ebisu Tower. *Tick tick tickety tick* went my nails on the tiny Blackberry keys as I would cruise towards the office. I was sure I would win a competition for Fastest Blackberry Typist if there was one; it might just compensate for the soreness in my thumb joints. I would usually start to feel nauseous halfway back to the office, and look up to check where we were. Perhaps it was the lack of sleep that made me carsick. I did not have the drive to appreciate the beautiful greenery through the taxi windows, and instead would keep my focus on the small screen. My neck would ache and I would feel queasy, but I soon figured that I would not throw up if I ignored the urge.

I normally managed to stumble back into the office and start the paperwork just as my colleagues flooded out to go home. I would decide at midnight that it was time to go home, and would hail another taxi, hop in, and take a nap during the journey.

I would frequently arrive home to realise that I had forgotten about meeting my friends for dinner. This happened so often that my friends became exasperated, and the number of accusatory texts – "Again?" – after my profuse apologies for missing dinner dwindled down to nothing. Eventually they blatantly ignored my absence. I would find solace in the custom of putting the kettle on before popping into the shower. Wrapped in my fluffy bathrobe, I would then gulp down another cup of spicy Korean noodles. And thus, another day.

I thrived on the hustle and hectic rhythm of my new job. I woke up every day excited to be in the office, solving some issue or question from other offices. I was exhausted, but I had fun. I remember when I was only 26 years old and I would have lunch with the Managing Director of a global insurance company – or the Corporate Treasurer of an investment bank. Whoever it was at any, it was always somebody important. It felt cool and convinced me that I was important. To the outsider it would seem that we were talking in sophisticated jargon as we gave our opinions about the Financial Times' reporting. It looked like we were turning the gears of the financial economy. Despite not understanding the meaning of my work, or how I fit into jigsaw puzzle of the huge financial industry, I was proud of myself. I tricked myself into feeling important, and that made sacrificing my health worth it.

Beneath the fragile surface, my spirit was eroding. I did not know what enjoying life was all about. Between work, meeting friends, going to the gym, going to the spa, shopping, dinners out, dates, drinks in Roppongi, studying for a master's degree and keeping in touch with people on Facebook, I thought I had the perfectly balanced life. The problem was, I did not even know what made me happy in the first place. I went through the motions to create the life I thought was my dream.

People come and people go in the expatriate world, and it often felt like a constant cycle of meeting new people and saying goodbye a few months later. There would be a few I would get close to for a few months, but who would then drift off for some strange reason. I would never hear from them again, however hard I tried to maintain contact. But of course, there were a precious few who stuck around – the kind who would check in and bring me chicken soup when I was down with another cold.

My raging thirst for power coaxed me to continue working even when the sniffles came about again. It was getting so frequent that eventually my girlfriends stopped making me chicken soup. My immune system was cracking with insufficient rest and my energy was draining. But I torpedoed on, getting out and about, networking and learning.

I wore the label of "expatriate" like a badge of honour. This was a dynamic world that I was fortunate to participate in and influence in some small way. I was condescending towards others who travelled less than me or – God forbid – did not travel at all. I thought it superficial to return to the same city 10 times a year to go shopping. Why did they not want to learn more about new cities and new things, and meet new people like I did? Why didn't they want to travel to a different city every holiday?

Sadly, as it turned out, I was rather lost in this world of mine. I did not know where I belonged. I was uncertain as to whether I was still part of Hong Kong, where I grew up and my parents resided, or if I was more at home within the cyber interface of Facebook and Twitter. What is this mish-mash of identity we develop after moving around? Where do we belong? Ask any expatriate, 'Where is home for you?' and you will more often than not get a few awkward moments of silence, a slight stammer, and then – because they have moved around so much – the cliché answer: 'Home is where the heart is.'

I had my doubts about being a permanent expatriate, but the colourful life it afforded me was a lot to give up. Did I want to be an expatriate forever, as my work contract stipulated? Abraham Maslow, the American Psychologist who devised Maslow's hierarchy of needs and personal development, would tell me I had failed at the stage of reaching a sense of belonging. Wherever we are, we all need to feel wanted, needed, and involved in some sort of community. I was involved in expatriate clubs and volunteer associations, helped organise charity balls and events, and was well-known in the foreign circle – but was this city my home?

I revered the expatriate life but did not know the harm it was doing to my body and soul. For a while, I prided myself on being geographically mobile and open-minded, but uprooting my life every few years was more stressful on the psyche than I expected. I developed a disillusioned sense of belonging when I settled into each new city. I thought I had mastered the language, the nuances, the history, and the culture, but a subtle gesture or a simple comment from a local friend made it clear that integrating was not as simple as knowing when to slurp noodles from a soup bowl. Expats never truly belonged, wherever they lived.

Our original homes have abandoned those who hide behind the entrancing jet-setting life. Work hard, play hard. Whenever I went back to Hong Kong, I was at loss for the current slang, the most popular TV shows, and what was considered "cool." I felt as if society had not progressed, and that seemingly miniscule problems brought people to the streets to protest. I wondered why people were more concerned over a government official's mistress than they were about the dying children and abandoned elderly in the poorer areas of Hong Kong. Either way, there was a serious disconnect. What was once home for me now felt like Atlantis.

In fact, we expats are all homeless bodies in limbo, for we are neither here nor there. Some feel slightly lost in this wasteland. I was utterly confused and felt like I had been cast off into a vacuum. I could get one foot in the door of different social groups, but never managed to get both feet in, let alone the whole person.

Ironically then, I had no sense of belonging according to Maslow's terms, despite having achieved world citizenship and a thick slab of visas stuck on my passport. I consoled myself by reaping transferable assets as I moved around, such as learning the local languages, to compensate for these aimless pursuits. This was both reason and rationalisation: adding languages to my CV would make me look more employable and indispensable. Languages are a window into culture and history. I loved learning them at school and thought about studying linguistics and anthropology, but my mother would have had a heart attack if I had insisted on doing those subjects at university. Instead I relented and chose to take on the two degrees of law and political science instead.

I was professional, elegant, calm, clear, and poised. I had a polished disguise so glossy in its veneer that even I came to believe that it was the real me. I embodied every inch of my mask. I could not let my colleagues see that I was petrified at client meetings, or that I was incognisant of how the trading markets worked. I couldn't let it show that I did not understand the macroeconomics of oil prices. I could not let people see me tremble at cocktail parties, unsure of how to approach strangers and leave a good impression. I couldn't disclose how insecure I felt wearing a full matching suit, because that would defeat the purpose of power dressing (to exude confidence and executive presence in greyish blue, navy blue, blue with white stripes, dark blue, and sky blue).

I had been groomed to be grown up from such an early age. I could not let people down now.

I accomplished my goals, which were even more colossal and spectacular than expected. Yet I was overwhelmed.

I adopted a self-righteous attitude with an illusion of a higher calling I had to fulfil. But I lacked purpose.

Unconsciously, I hid the childlike side of me, tucking the soft toys and ornaments away in my apartment, hiding them from view during house parties. I kept up the façade.

*Let me continue to live my life for others, until it takes my last breath away.*

**Figure 2:** *Noisie.*

*Noisie has an artists' personality; he expresses himself through music and bangs around. No one appreciates the noise he makes, but he is convinced one day his melodies and creation will be understood by the world.*

# CHAPTER 2

# INVINCIBLE

The day before I started to crumble in 2009, I had an important client meeting. I was now in Beijing, having moved here from Tokyo. I did not want to fail anyone, least of all this new team here in Beijing. Disappointment was not in my repertoire, and I imagined my mother's stern, critical eyes boring into me. I heard her demanding that I pick myself up and act strong. I pretended to be engaged in what the client had to say, nodding my head at 10-second intervals. With stubborn willpower, I kept my feet firmly grounded, even though I was on the verge of walking out from the presentation. My head had started reeling and I could feel the start of a hammering on the back of my head, thudding lightly.

The meeting finally ended. I could feel the last drops of my energy drying up as I shook the CEO's hand goodbye, promising a proposal by the end of the day with a weak smile. I remained silent on the car ride back to the office while my colleague chirped on about the meeting. As we got back to the office, I kept my cool and told him, with as much politeness I could muster, to draft something legible for my approval. Then I escaped to my dismal cubicle.

Dark green stars began to appear on my computer screen as I struggled to focus. My head thumped. I felt nausea creeping up my gut. The office walls caved in, sucking out the oxygen reserved for me. I wanted to cry. Luckily the rest of the office had gone to lunch and did not witness my breakdown. I scribbled a note to my boss and attached the sick leave letter I had been carrying in my handbag for the last 10 days, not wanting to succumb to my physical weakness. I called my driver to pick me up.

Once I got home I flung off my heels, tore off my navy-blue suit, and hopped into the shower. The hot water soothed my head, but the pain refused to dissipate entirely. I decided to take a nap and wait for Timmie to come home. As I dried my hair I peered at myself in the mirror. My complexion was muddy green and my eyes stared lifelessly from their bony sockets, enveloped by bruised purple circles. My dimples were gone. My hair hung like broken twigs from a dying tree. It was a frightful sight and I dared not look at myself any longer. I put on my nightgown and sat on my bed.

Tears started rolling down my cheeks. I couldn't control my sobbing. Overwhelming fatigue engulfed my body.

The migraines had started the second weekend after I moved from Tokyo to Beijing. That should have been a stronger warning than the frequent stomach aches I'd had previously. I had sloughed through the first week of work, getting to know the people, the politics, the factions. The team had seemed friendly enough, and I ignored the discomfort of the office (a matchbox space tucked away in an immense commercial building, where the sharp fluorescent lights threw garish colours onto the grey, carpeted floor). I had a corner cubicle just next to the window through which the sun glared around three o'clock in the afternoon. The office was on the other side of town from my hotel. Traffic was hideous in Beijing, and I would be stuck in a foul taxi for an hour just to travel 15 kilometres. Eventually I'd started splashing out on a driver and a car.

By the time I had got back to the hotel that second Friday evening, my head had been aching for a few hours. I had dismissed it as one of those small headaches that will pass if you ignore it long enough; sometimes I could even will it away. As a prevention, I had popped two Panadol pills to hopefully gain some uninterrupted sleep.

I had woken suddenly at midnight, screaming in pain. My head was pounding, I could not see clearly, and I was sweating and gasping for breath. I took two more painkillers and tried hard to go back to sleep. By three o'clock in the morning, I was tossing and turning in excruciating pain. I fumbled through the documents I had brought with me and threw the file onto the floor until I saw the insurance emergency card peeking out. With trembling hands, I called and asked for a doctor. I was sobbing and crying uncontrollably, and the operator kept telling me to calm down and take deep breaths.

I had then gone down to the hotel reception and asked them to take me to the clinic, but they said there was a nearby hospital with an expatriate section. I was too weak to argue. The guard half-carried me to a Chinese hospital around the corner, where the garish lights made me vomit. The doctor I saw was a brash woman who told me she couldn't do much, and that I'd have to wait until six o'clock in the morning to see a neurologist. I was getting impatient as the pain snowballed. I felt alone and helpless. I stumbled out of the hospital, demanded my money back, and asked to be brought back to the hotel.

The next morning, I found my way to the clinic I had originally wanted to go to. I saw the doctor on duty who treated me properly – like a person. And it was in that consultation room that I learnt the word for my headaches: migraine.

I read up on migraines afterwards, and a simple Google search led me to Wikipedia, which said:

"A migraine is a chronic neurological disorder characterized by recurrent headaches that are moderate to severe. The typical migraine headache is unilateral (affecting one half of the head), pulsating in nature, and lasts from two to 72 hours. Symptoms include nausea, vomiting, photophobia (increased sensitivity to light) and phonophobia (increased sensitivity to sound). The word derives from the Greek hemikrania, 'pain on one side of the head'".[9]

The term for the white light in front of my eyes during the migraine was "aura", which sounded strange to me; I had always thought that "aura" had a positive connotation.

I slept all that weekend. On the Monday morning I was still writhing and wailing in pain, but I went back to the office as usual, willing myself to ignore it. I spoke cheerfully on conference calls even though I could have screamed from the piercing headache.

As if by military training, the migraine had arrived at precisely 3.03pm every afternoon after that. I felt like seven bulldozers had moved in on my head at the same time. The monthly stomach aches and colds I'd had while working in Tokyo paled in comparison. Even the exorbitant amounts I'd paid for deep tissue massages when working in Paris seemed worth it.

Nothing had improved even after a month had passed. I cried from the pain and banged my head against the wall to make the throbbing go away. The doctor started giving me stronger painkillers. I had every CT scan done, saw every specialist possible. Blood vessels were swollen in my head but there were no apparent causes – or at least, none that I believed.

There was one that I did not want to believe, and that I would vehemently deny: my inability to cope with stress.

I relied on my obstinate belief in myself that I was invincible, that I was strong, that I could get through all the challenges myself. I willed the migraines away.

And so, after that fateful diagnosis at the start of my stay in Beijing, I would wake up so many mornings with groans of despair. The anticipation I had once had for the day ahead had surreptitiously turned into agony. I had tantrums, cursing my suits and catapulting my heels at the door before stomping out to get to work. I had expected to be ecstatic about the novelty and challenge with my move to Beijing, but was instead consumed by apathy. Daily pulsating migraines killed whatever enthusiasm was left. I was furious with myself for not being more upbeat, more collected, and more energetic.

The pain made me cry all the time. I hated my life. I thought I was indomitable and nothing could crush me.

The doctor also gave me the strongest painkillers she could prescribe for my migraines and suggested I take sick leave for a month to rest. She told me these pills were one stop short of morphine injections.

I dismissed all the warnings from these physical symptoms. I was stubborn and believed in the fantasy that I had it all – an expatriate package with a multinational company, youth, enthusiasm, friends, health, relationships, a promising future – as was the jargon. Once I earned X amount and was promoted to global head of a business, then I would take some time off, travel, and cuddle up leisurely on my couch to read my dusty collection of Dr Seuss books. Why rock the boat now?

I underestimated my environment and overestimated my capacity to cope.

**Figure 3:** Lurkie.
*Lurkie is a triple agent with a strong, invincible image. Lurkie spies on other bears. He tries to make a name for himself by doing something great, so charges around with a self-imposed sense of importance and urgency. He is confused about the meaning of his work and looking for his place in Beardom. Behind the veneer of vigour, he is shy and just wants to be loved.*

# CHAPTER 3

# DEFRAGMENTATION

Winter came early to Beijing that year. I wore only a skimpy nightgown, and I could feel the wind whipping at my legs.

I'd moved back to Beijing from Tokyo a few months ago. It seemed so far away. Paris was history. The first snow had fallen on Halloween, an ominous warning for the cold, dreary months ahead.

Tonight's chill was numbing. I sat on my bedroom window ledge, legs dangling over the city. The frosty wind bit my toes, but I felt no pain. Extreme hopelessness had brought me to an eerie peace.

My resolve was unwavering. The only doubt I had left was whether jumping from the sixth floor would ensure me an instant death. I did not want to risk ending up paralysed, in a coma, or crippled for life. It would have to be a fatal leap.

There was rationality in the irrationality.

I was immersed in melancholy, nonbeing, and anguish.

Nothing interested me anymore – not clothes, make-up, sex, or novels. Not even food.

Instead, I had become shrouded in self-loathing, self-pity, and disappointment in myself. These proved to be near-fatal thoughts, all of which spiralled into different directions. I had seen a psychologist, who had put me on antidepressants after diagnosing me with severe major depression.

I was desperate to escape, but I didn't know what from. I didn't know where I could run to. I felt like my mind was trapped under 50 feet of snow – an avalanche of depression.

I was waving like mad to get people to see me and help me out of the wretchedness in which I was entangled, but they just smiled and waved back. They didn't hear me screaming; they could only see the successful façade that I presented to the world.

I was frantic, but it felt as though the avalanche only buried me further when I tried to escape it.

For too many months I had been lifeless, sprawled out in bed, curtains drawn shut 24 / 7 so that I could hide from the light. I didn't eat much and lost about 10 kilos. I didn't leave the house.

It was ridiculous for me to be frustrated, because I'd put my faith in this glamorous illusion I'd created for the world to see. But really, I saw no meaning in it. I was hurting inside, I was weary, and I had no energy for anything. I no longer had the ambition to go after promotions; I wasn't interested in seeing the Northern Lights or visiting Machu Picchu anymore. I saw no purpose in my insignificant existence on Earth. The façade of happiness was peeling away. Was I supposed to stay alive to make more money to put into a pensions account? Or to make it to Director?

Maybe my usual technique of devouring tubs of ice cream could save me from this prolonged melancholy. But there was no ice cream left in the fridge.

I ached to put an end to this misery. I peered over my knees and saw a car turning into the driveway. I grasped the window frame and leaned my head further out. The icy air tempted me to ride its current into the void. I edged out so only the end of my buttocks were touching the ledge. My legs fought against gravity, which was pulling me down millimetre by millimetre. Minutes passed, and then I released my fingers from the window frame and closed my eyes. An uncanny serenity flowed over my mind and body. I felt myself floating through the air for a split second.

Then I crashed into the set of drawers next to the window.

My boyfriend Timmie had arrived home and run into the room at the exact second my fingers had uncurled from the steel frame. I had not even heard him come in. He caught me by my waist and dragged me in. The momentum threw both of us to the floor and I hit my head on the drawers.

He carried me to the bed, laid me down gently, and rocked me in his arms for a few moments. I felt like a helpless infant. I started sobbing again. He ran his fingers through my hair, hushed me with a lullaby, and went to lock the windows.

I curled into a ball. I laid there and cried myself to sleep, hoping that would cure my depression. For months, depression had clamped down tightly and leeched every ounce of energy out of me. But I wanted to rip it off and get rid of it. Until I had started taking antidepressants, I did not know that depression was an illness, and a deadlier one than most people realised. Sixty per cent of suicides around the world were correlated to depressive symptoms, according to the World Health Organization and American Psychological Association. Each day, there are over 300 million people on the planet suffering from depression. By 2020, depression will be the top "disease burden" in the world – i.e. a condition with which one lives for years – ahead of more commonly understood conditions such as heart attacks and cancer. Depression is ranked by WHO as the single largest contributor to global disability. Stress and burnout are now recognised to be triggering causes of depression[10].

Depression is a deep-rooted issue in all parts of the world, more prevalent than most people imagine. Only in the last 10 years have Western countries such as the US, UK and Australia become more open to increasing awareness about the illness, or even recognised it as a medical condition. In many other countries, and especially in Asia, the taboo around depression is a big one, for having depression denotes weakness, defect, and loss of face.

Contrary to a still widely held public opinion, clinical depression is no joke, and not a naïve state out of which one can snap with a shake of the shoulder. Depression is a mood disorder in which mood and motivation are lower than usual for a prolonged period, with other symptoms ranging from – but not limited to – loss of appetite, loss of sex drive, insomnia, hallucinations and delusions. The risk of suicide for a person suffering from depression is exceptionally high, with depression being the major contributor to suicide numbers. According to the WHO[11] there are close to 800,000 suicides globally per year. However, less than half of those who suffer from depression, regardless of gender, seek help. At least twice as many may not even be aware that they suffer from the condition.

None of these statistics meant anything to me a few years back. The list of symptoms in the *Diagnostic and Statistical Manual of Mental Disorders* was only a string of letters.

The report from my clinical psychologist read like an epitaph on a tombstone:

- lacking motivation
- visualising killing herself
- attempting to cut her wrists but unable to carry it out
- increasingly negative thoughts, especially when alone
- tired of job and has lost interest, just too routine
- history of depressed mood
- self-alienating, not wanting to interact
- poor sleeping habits
- lots of ruminating

- outlook on life changed, conflicted
- appetite waning, eats bland food and has no motivation to eat
- parental issues

I ignored my depressed state for almost a year and would kid myself on a daily basis that the next day I would manage to get to work and fly to Shanghai from Beijing for business trips. I was unable to come to terms with it – I just could not grasp the idea.

So I devoted my energy to solving my migraines and physical pain, things that were, in comparison, more real and tangible. I felt like I was a weakling when depressed. I went to see a brain specialist in Hong Kong. They saw me for 15 minutes, asked about my history, charged me an exorbitant amount, and sent me on my way with a sagacious suggestion to Timmie: 'Please treat the depression first.'

With that, I decided the specialist was a phony, and tried other experts.

The neurologist did a few balance exercises with me, like stretching my hands up in the air and touching my toes. Did I feel dizzy? No? I was fine. I met with an Ear, Nose and Throat specialist to get rid of the ringing in my ears. He suspected I had vertigo problems, but that wasn't curable. The optometrist told me my eyesight was perfect. All three specialists informed me that the paramount priority was to treat my depression first.

About six months after I arrived in Beijing – and following a long trail of migraines – my doctors had unanimously suggested that I take a month's sick leave from work. I was insistent at first about being able to manage my work amidst the pain and depressive moods, but when I woke up one night after dreaming of drowning myself, I knew I couldn't force it anymore. So, day after day, I rotted at home, musing about my pitiful existence. I was so incompetent, I thought, that I couldn't even kill myself.

Why had the success I had built up in the 28 years of my life fallen apart?

When had I started to derail from the set-for-success track I had followed so strictly?

**Figure 4:** *Fuzzie.*
*Fuzzie is a banker bear. He's stressed out reading the Financial Times and Bloomberg every day. He is extremely calculative and will only do favours if he thinks he will get good favours in return in the future.*

# CHAPTER 4

# SUPER PERFECT

'Not good enough!'

Most children who grew up in a Chinese household know that phrase all too well. Hearing that was our worst nightmare.

That phrase thundered through my brain over and over again as I lay idle with depression. I was stuck in Beijing, for I had nowhere else to go. I had been given generous sick leave from my company to sort myself out. I was on antidepressants and undergoing psychotherapy. Memories that had lain dormant for nearly 20 years surged to the forefront of my mind. Day after day, I tried to understand why I was going through this. I gasped for breath while Timmie held me and stroked my hair.

'I am not good enough,' I sobbed. 'That's why I'm depressed. I am not good enough, not strong enough.'

Biting my lip, eyes downcast, I decided to resign from my job, admitting that I was not good enough to go back to the office. I was scared to see my colleagues and I was too ill to be functional. I needed a clean break.

The decision brought temporary relief. I called my parents, who lived in Hong Kong, to give them an update. I was naïve to expect any reassurance to come down that phone line. They fired questions at me like bullets from an automatic machine gun, striking down the last slice of energy left in me.

'Why are you depressed? What is wrong with you? Why are you so weak?'

'It is a good company and you have a good contract. They will take care of you and your family! Why are you stupid enough to give it away?'

'Others would die for your contract! Be grateful!'

'What will you do afterwards if you quit?'

'Why are you not strong enough to overcome this and go back to work?'

'You cannot just stay at home. Migraines are nothing ...'

An auntie I spoke to showed no sympathy at all. 'What reason do you have to be depressed? You have everything!'

Surely there must be life after a corporate career? Maybe gemology or something like that. Or study. Or travel. Why did it have to be a job? Why did I have to look for another job? I didn't know what I would do. I was confused, lost, with no idea what my compass was set to if it was no longer pointing to society's magnetic north.

This was too much for anyone to accept; I was the antithesis of every flawless child who is groomed to be perfect in Hong Kong.

The painful pulsing in my head threatened to overtake me, and I cried all night like a toddler in a frenzy. Timmie could only look on and ensure that I didn't hit myself as I kicked the coffee table and threw cushions at the bookshelf.

All my life, I believed that the purpose of my existence was to achieve and meet the standards set by society, my parents, teachers, and the media. Everyone else but myself. In school I would run home with a story about something that had happened at school that day – for instance, coming second in a book report competition in junior high school.

Instead of an exclamation of glee and pride, I heard: 'Why did you not come first?' My efforts were rebuffed, not good enough. 'Why can't you be more like Jessica, who always gets 100% on her exams?' my parents would ask.

Not even my looks measured up. The list of criticisms grew all the time: my nose was too big, my thighs too fat, my waist too long, my skin too tan.

When Amy Chua's book on Tiger Mothers[12] was published, many were stunned to find out that Chinese mothers forced their children to practise piano for five hours a day in order to get into the most prestigious performing arts schools or recitals. The underlying premise of the Tiger Mother's parenting strategies is to be strict, disciplined, and persistent, which was the norm in Hong Kong, where I grew up.

Now, "Tiger Mother" implies a style of authoritarian parenting – both by fathers and mothers – that requires full and undivided obedience, emphasises strict discipline and punishment, employs an emphasis on titles, competitions, and status, and offers little praise for awards less than first place. Chinese mothers have been broadly stereotyped because of Chua's book. Although not all of them are Tiger Mothers, the vast majority are. The general consensus sees the Tiger Mother as an authoritative regime of absolute obedience. The merit of Tiger Mother parenting is proven by awards, Ivy League degrees *cum laude,* admission to elite boarding school, contracts with Fortune 500 companies, weighty pay checks, and expensive cars.

Tiger Mothering is not just limited to Asian or Chinese people, however. In countries like the UK, children are routinely pushed to study hard for advanced placements, and to achieve the highest percentiles in their SATS and Advanced Level examinations. This alone isn't sufficient, however, and children are moulded into maths whizzes and violin prodigies.

In the US, the push towards the Ivy League schools begins earlier each year, with American parents enrolling their toddlers into expensive kindergartens, which allegedly develop children to become smarter and more accomplished. This is in preparation for college applications a decade later.

I saw with my own eyes – while I was an undergraduate exchange student in one of the *grandes écoles* in Paris – how the French students, vying for entrance to these prestigious schools, studied more hours than investment bankers, devoting the last drop of midnight oil into their *prépas* (endless test drills and regurgitation of facts about international relations dating back to when dinosaurs roamed the earth).

Tiger Mothers – and Fathers – are everywhere.

They mean well, of course. They want to give the best to their children in order for them to be successful. What is perhaps not so understood, however, is that these Tiger Mothers often had destitute childhoods, and their lack of opportunities and education ring loud and clear in the back of their minds. Hence the desperate transference onto little beings like me, so that the next generation can right their parents' wrongs. Tiger Parents live vicariously through us. They do what they think is best at the time with the best of intentions, though their actions are perhaps misguided or too extreme.

While we now have understanding and empathy towards our Tiger Mothers, it is nevertheless important that we process our own childhood experiences. Experiences and memories are almost always subjective. A child's fragmented memories of events and statements could help us understand what elements have led to their depression and, at times, their arrogance, sense of entitlement, and illusions of grandeur.

Children churned out by Tiger Mothers usually grow up to be successful by society's standards. By the time they reach their early twenties, they have graduated from a prestigious university, are laden with accolades, and have made their parents proud. Well-groomed and disciplined, Tiger Cubs do not entertain the possibility of failure, and appear at all times to be contented with their lives. After all, how could one complain about perfection?

For people like me who grew up in Hong Kong, the rat race starts as early as kindergarten, where kids feel the pressure to attain perfect grades. Tiger Mothers push children to perform and adorn CVs with extracurricular activities that signal the right attributes to prospective future employers. A two-year-old may get a star for being able to share, signifying social skills advantageous to working in a team. Why don't parents realise that "sharing" is such an abstract concept for a toddler to grasp? That demanding a child should share is ludicrous? When every parent is yelling 'share, share, share' in playgroups, we must yield to the pressure. Suffice to say, for many of Hong Kong's children, there was not a lot of time for fun and play, for it was deemed unproductive.

I had nothing to complain about either. I was organised, planned, decisive, determined. I managed my time efficiently. I practised hard and improved each time. I finished all my homework before I got home.

I strived to be perfect and to win every competition. I went through loads of rote learning and can now recite poems from Tang Dynasty because they were drilled into me (although I have absolutely no idea what they mean, nor do I understand the references made to the political situation at that time). I was able to recite multiplication tables upon entry to primary school – three times three is nine, four times four is 16 etc. I could write Chinese characters with calligraphy brushes, pirouette, and read stories out loud with a posh British accent. I knew that Q came after P in the alphabet.

Every new bit of education I received tarnished my creativity and imagination: knowledge, structure, logic, the correct way to write a memo, an official letter, or a postcard! This is where subjects go in a sentence, these are gerunds, transitive verbs, and past participles in the English language. This was all important knowledge – important information – all at the expense of creative writing, doodling, staring off into space, and playing hopscotch.

There was too much homework. There were exercise drills, cursive writing lessons. Do not, I repeat, DO NOT draw out of the line! Do not colour outside of the box. Follow the colour scheme by number codes. This is how to draw a dog.

I wanted to draw a space dog. Not allowed. I would get a D for my art class.

I wanted to paint with my fingers. Not allowed. It was stencil sketch class.

I wanted to write about frogs and aliens with bulging eyes. Okay, that might have been tolerated, as long as I used some of the new vocabulary we had highlighted, learnt and repeatedly written so that we would know it by heart for our weekly dictations.

Reading was a good habit to have – but not fantasy and fiction. We read *Good King Wenceslas* and Wide Range Readers. The stories had morals in them. I started reading *The Economist* in junior high school, since martial arts kung fu novels or the *Sweet Valley High* series were considered to squander my intellect.

The emphasis on rote learning – the pressure to write, to repeat, to do what we were *supposed* to do – meant that the chance to discover and imagine beyond what was prescribed was forgone. Tests and examinations were much more important. And rightly so. How else would we tell the good from the bad, the intelligent from the dull, the successful from the failures, out in the real world where the competition was so fierce?

This in itself is an issue, because it is as if these were the only labels for us. A dichotomy. Right or wrong. Good or bad. Make it in life, or be forgotten.

Play was seen as a waste of time. No one really believes that playing could help 16-year-old students spit out accurate answers during merciless public examinations that define their future!

As a child I created my own book with crayons and published a story of a caterpillar with too many legs. But I soon buried attempts to emulate Hemingway when I took the advice of teachers and parents who suggested I study something more practical, like law, to ensure a respectable career. I excelled on the trajectory laid out for me at the expense of my passion for writing. I charged head-on too quickly. I forgot to simply live. No wonder I was unhappy.

Discontent came in the form of abandoning what I desired, such as playing basketball and hanging out with friends after practice. My mother thought it was a waste of time. One year, I was banned from basketball practice for a few months in case I sprained my fingers, which might have hindered me in my piano examination. In silent revenge, I failed the piano examination on purpose by playing as many wrong notes I could. I made a mess of the offering music by forgetting my music score.

But imperfection was not to be tolerated. My mother signed me up for another piano exam the following year, and in the meantime, I could play basketball again. It was a small triumph on my side. I did scrape a pass on my Grade 8 piano examinations, but so what? I'm not quite sure how that added to my life, except to make me detest Bach and Wagner – not because I don't like their music, but because they remind me of my harrowing experience at the piano. The same piano stands in my apartment today, quiet, covered, and despised. I only ever touched it to play nursery rhymes for my children.

I was not permitted to throw tantrums, and I could not cry in public. My manners were as polished as a socialite's before I turned 10. I was not allowed to touch drugs, alcohol or cigarettes, and never "messed up" during my teenage years. There was no time for experimentation; I was too busy cramming in theories of momentum and memorising the human anatomy in preparation for being the doctor I didn't want to become. My mother suffered no loss of face due to teenage pregnancy, abortion, or other "shameful" behaviours in our family. I was rebellious in mind and attitude, though subservient. Obedience covered up the anger and rage, for to express these emotions was unacceptable and would risk me being thrown out of the family – or so I thought when I was locked outside the apartment as punishment for my sins.

I was not under the same delusion as my mother, and I knew I was not the elite student she boasted about in front of her friends. I therefore worked extra hard to fulfil the image she created. I started to internalise their expectations so that they became *my* (sometimes irrationally high) expectations. I not only had to do my best in academics, but in sports, in debate, in everything I was involved in. I trained as much as I could until my arms and legs were trembling with fatigue and muscle pains. I hammered out my speech letter by letter and practised so many times to make sure I was going to nail it. I became competitive. I compared myself to everyone else. Bronze trophies and medals were not enough – I wanted gold. I wanted to be first – I *had* to be first. I wanted to show them, show everyone that I could do it. I could reach my potential – the potential that everyone thought I had, but I could never see. I became the ultimate person.

And then the only person I disappointed was myself.

I became an overachiever. Extreme perfectionism was the only right way to live, and to avoid the "not good enough" verdict. The paradox is that this mindset made me inadequate in everything, because perfection is impossible. I had given myself an insufferable curse.

To prevent this sense of disappointment, I worked hard. I studied. I practised. If I became the best, I reasoned, my parents and teachers would stop criticising me and I could finally do what I loved. The gradual accumulation of awards and prizes fuelled my determination, and also built my internal strength and confidence.

However, this outward confidence I exhibited was deceptive. I was mistaken for an overly ambitious young woman, and the fake zeal masked my insecurities and rage. I did as I was told, succumbing to external pressure from teachers, parents, and peers, but I felt like a nobody. Dreams were forgotten as I began to abide by the rules I saw set out in front of me, too scared to find an alternative, not knowing there could be alternatives. Emotions and responses seen as negative and weak were suppressed. I became proud, self-righteous, and disillusioned.

By the time my fellow Tiger Cubs have been in the workforce for five years, they have likely been subjected to consistent performance pressure for 20 years. This pressure begins to take its toll and shows up in physical ailments such as headaches and regular colds. Chatting to my Tiger Cub friends, we wondered, what if we were allowed to pursue our dreams?

The heart-wrenching fact of the matter was that no one remembered their childhood dreams, for we had forgotten them in the process of building a life of luxury to be envied by others. Most of my friends are now married with children, and will continue to work in their stale, secure jobs to pay off the 20-year mortgage that they took out in order to own an apartment. This scenario has become their goal, their passion, and their identity.

All this accumulated mental stress was worse than all of the physical punishment added up together. It took me 30 years to realise the impact my childhood experiences had on my psyche. Studies have shown a correlation between the Tiger Mother parenting method and mental health issues such as depression, anxiety and even suicide.

I can attest to the potency of life as a Tiger Cub. As Alice Miller wrote in *The Drama of the Gifted Child*[13], so many children were admired and envied for being mature and successful at a young age, but behind this lurked depression, a feeling of emptiness and the sense that their lives had no meaning.

Mike Vilensky wrote in *New York Magazine* that the cost of a rigid timetable of activities imposed by parents is a loss of creativity[14]. Indeed, this is one of the greatest tragedies of the Tiger Cub childhood. Creativity is not simply arts and crafts; it is a different way of thinking, a perspective beyond our imagination. This is often why creative minds land top positions at global corporations; they create a world not previously imagined, such as those innovated by Bill Gates, Arianna Huffington, Zhang Xin, and many other entrepreneurs. People who do what they love. People who did not have creativity weaned out of them during their upbringing.

Asian schooling, particularly that in China, is distinctive in that it emphasises regurgitation of facts and knowledge. My schooling in Hong Kong was no exception. There are set model answers even for English composition writing, where one would assume imagination and creativity were allowed. Children are expected to finish at 4.00pm and then devote their remaining waking hours to homework every day. In order to get ahead, many are enrolled in after-school tuition classes, which means that children could not even start their homework until 9 or 10 o'clock at night. Parents assumed that practice makes perfect. There are public examinations every few years. Places for the top schools are competitive. There, students are taught by more qualified – sometimes expatriate – teachers and form a large number of those admitted to the top universities across the world.

Oliver James, British psychologist and author of Affluenza[15], wrote about the lack of creativity as a major problem in Asian schools. His research, based on imagining doubling your salary, showed the lack of imagination of Asian students. "They were simply incapable of picturing an abstract situation and of entering into a game," noted James. "I am sure this was because their creativity had been systematically destroyed and, in its place, a survival pragmatism installed."

I was more than pragmatic in my choices: would being on the debate team help me get into the Hong Kong mooting team, which would make me sound more potent for law firm recruiters? It is no wonder that I do not know to love unconditionally, for everything was conditional upon a return on investment.

A BBC article in 2011 – which discussed the notion that Tiger Mothers underestimate the cognitive difficulty of certain activities – quotes New York Times columnist David Brooks, who argues that sleepovers are actually more intellectually demanding than music practice. "Managing status rivalries, negotiating group dynamics, understanding social norms, navigating the distinction between self and group – these and other social tests impose cognitive demands that blow away any intense tutoring session or a class at Yale."[16]

I did not learn this at the age of 14, and so had to do so at the age of 34.

Society continues to kill us. In 2017 alone, Hong Kong saw almost 100 school students die by suicide. The rate is not slowing down in 2018. Notes left behind described the immense examination pressure, the push to excel, and the shame students felt when they could not, did not, achieve their parents' expectations. One painful newspaper report cut through me like a knife: a mother was reported to be berating her primary school child for the low marks in an examination, and apparently said, 'Even if you kill yourself, I will burn homework for you to do in hell!'[17] I say that the mother can go to hell herself.

Research indicates that high-achieving Tiger Cubs are more likely to suffer from depression and stress than their European-American counterparts. This is a result of the Tiger Mother parenting style[18]. According to Desiree Baolian Qin, a professor in the Department of Human Development and Family Studies at Michigan State University, strict parenting[19] and stellar academic achievement are common in Chinese immigrant families. But unfortunately, so are depression and stress.

Qin found that academia was an enormous point of contention in Chinese-American families. The students complained that their parents talked constantly about academics and reacted emotionally to failure[20]. 'They just take everything so literally, and exaggerate,' one female student told Qin. 'Like if I get one bad grade, they think, "Oh no, you're going to fail school; you're going to become one of those bad girls who do drugs.'"

Students also struggled with being compared to other children or family members, such as an older sibling who went to an Ivy League university.

One success meant moving on to the next one. There was no time to celebrate – the future was at our heels.

I was always planning for the future. In kindergarten I was preparing for junior school, in junior school I was preparing for high school. By the age of 12, I was thinking about how to build my resumé for university applications. In high school I was preparing for exams and doing all sorts of activities to get a rounded education so I could apply to the top universities in the world, thereby increasing the chance to get a good job with a high income. I went to the top girls' school in Hong Kong, many alumni of which were well-known and successful in all sectors. Many went to Ivy League universities. I wanted to be one of them, so I kept pushing myself.

In university I had to start building a CV again so that big firms and corporates would take me on. On the very first day of university I was applying for scholarships and awards, auditioning for the debate and moot teams in order to build my credentials for job applications – job applications that I wouldn't be making for another four years.

I cannot blame society for warning us about the unknown and insuring us for the future. There is certain logic in saving part of my income for future expenditure instead of spending it all on shoes, handbags or alcohol. The problem is, like many things, I took planning for the future to the extreme.

*When I am 18 ...*

*When I grow up ...*

*I'll work hard now so I can benefit in the future ...*

*I'll save my money for the future. I won't spend now ...*

And when I started my job, I kept planning – for the promotion, the titles, the qualifications. I didn't think about the present; I was never "in the now". I was always thinking ahead, tomorrow, one week later, one year later, five years later, 20 years from now ... It was as if everything I did was for some distant end goal. Did I enjoy the activities I was involved in? I guess so – well, most of them, anyway. Were they simply for the sake of enjoyment or because they took my interest? I doubt it. Was I happy? I do not remember having the time to be happy or not. I was too engrossed in building for "the future".

I dared not slow down.

Analysing why my teachers' and parents' offhand remarks emasculated my tiny ego brought forth a self-understanding – in the same way that understanding why my mother did what she did brought forth empathy. I saw myself from her point of view, and knew she only wanted what was best for me. I realised that the Tiger Mother holds no malice against their Cubs. In fact, she loves her Cubs so much it suffocates them.

I internalised the "what is best for me" argument as if it was the ultimate truth, and that's what drove me. I sprinted down the track as fast as I could to reach one destination, only to then start the next race towards another finish line. I was stubbornly living for the future, when the past was still present. I ran too fast – faster than I could handle. It was a never-ending game and I exhausted myself.

Naturally, I tripped myself over.

It was not surprising that I got sick and stressed. And yet when I was on my IV drip at the hospital, I was worrying about the emails I had to send, the apples I needed to buy ...

And most of all, I worried about how to keep up the image of a successful woman in a corporate world. I needed to be CEO one day!

**Figure 5:** *Shittie.*

*Shittie defines himself as possibly the only white piece of shit in this world. On good days he asserts that it is his USP. On bad days, he questions his strangeness and pitifully admits that he doesn't fit into the inner circle of brown shits. He just wants to be seen, but is wrought with self-doubt. He feels like a "not-good-enough" piece of shit. Let's hope he doesn't hit the fan any time soon.*

# CHAPTER 5

# BURNOUT

The hardest thing was telling my company that I was dysfunctional and disabled from depression. This wasn't as simple as it would have been if I was declaring I had a brain tumour. I worried that they would think I was being lazy, as I had heard those comments said of others before me. I'd been promoted and had moved to Beijing after Tokyo, and my old regional boss had put his job on the line to help me get the posting to China. I had to perform well and repay their generosity. I felt I was letting him down by staying at home and wallowing in self-pity. I'd also taken to playing with bears, which was helping to calm my mind and distract me occasionally from my plight. How could anybody take my illness seriously?

I could not bear to be absent from work. I didn't want to be weak and I didn't want to fail.

My daily activity consisted of waking up in the middle of the day, getting out of bed, stumbling out to the living room in a dizzy fog, and collapsing onto the guest mattress until evening, when I could go back to my bed again. I had lost so much weight in just a few weeks because I could not eat. I had no desire for food, not even when steaming hot Thai green curry was placed in front of me.

I wasn't even sure why I needed antidepressants, or what depression even meant, so I googled it. I read website after website of symptoms and ways to get out of depression. I scoffed at the simplistic views these people had when explaining the experience. Did they really know what it was like to not be able to stop crying? Sometimes I would cry during every waking moment! I wanted to tear out the agony from inside me and flush it down the toilet. I did not understand where this excruciating distress was coming from.

Shouldn't I have been happy with the perfect life I had? What had I done to deserve this unexplainable, infernal agony? The websites told me to exercise more – as if I had any motivation by then. I couldn't even wash my face.

Doctors decided that my depression and migraines were caused by stress. I was distraught. The severity of my plight meant I was unfit for work, and I did not know how to explain it to anyone. I berated myself for not going to work and doing what I was sent there to do. I felt like I had let everyone down. I couldn't bear the fact that they knew I wasn't coping with life and work. I had explained to my hiring manager that I was sick and gave him the medical certificates, but I didn't explain anything in detail. The most I would talk about was about the migraines and the physical pains. I felt ashamed to have to mention depression. In the end, I did have to tell HR about the mental health situation as they had to process my sick leave days and other related insurance matters. To everyone else – the colleagues had worked with in different global offices, the other reporting managers, the clients – it appeared I had simply vanished.

However, the thought of needing to go back to work hung at the back of my mind. I couldn't find peace, but neither could I be bothered. I didn't know what my problem was. I had a good job and had been promoted quickly over the few years at the company. My colleagues loved me and I had cultivated a good reputation that I now seemed bent on destroying. I knew I ought to go back to the office; I just wanted to be out of this state of mind and become "normal" again. I was so scared that they might see me as weak or incompetent if I told them about the depression. So I hid away and avoided contact.

One in four people around us are thinking about killing themselves this very moment. Job stress is indeed one factor, but there may be other factors causing burnout and depression, such as family, hereditary reasons, and lack of coping mechanisms. The numbers are staggering. The World Economic Forum estimates that annually, being absent from the job (absenteeism) or underperforming while working (presenteeism) causes productivity losses worth 1.6 trillion US dollars due to mental health conditions[21].

The Australian Bureau of Statistics estimates that untreated mental health conditions cost Australian workplaces approximately 10.9 billion US dollars per year[22]. The US National Alliance on Mental Illness calculates an annual loss of 6,439 US dollars per employee in the US. Work disability (short-term and long-term disability insurance and days off work) costs 21 billion US dollars annually[23], with an average of 26 weeks of sick leave in duration[24]. Consequently, staff replacement to substitute for the ill – and turnover due to long-term illness – costs 3.4 billion US dollars annually[25]. This isn't even taking into account the hidden costs of low staff morale, low employee engagement, and stress. Furthermore, other physical illnesses could stem from depression, such as heart conditions, chronic fatigue, chronic neck and back pain, and obesity – thereby increasing the costs of medical insurance and treatment[26].

Depression is not the issue of the individual alone; it affects families, groups, companies and societies. Depression could also, at times, simply be the tip of the iceberg, an indication of much deeper issues such as domestic violence, trauma, and discrimination. For the individual, their depression could be a manifestation of burnout, a chronic fatigue triggered by stress from all different aspects of life.

Burnout can be caused by work-related issues and, at other times, personal issues. Burnout is a sense of being overwhelmed emotionally, physically, and mentally. It is a disproportionate weariness that could result in such physical ailments as strokes, heart attacks, and ulcers. Ultimately, it affects your functionality and your ability to work.

Still many companies choose to ignore this issue, shoving it in the pigeon holes of Diversity & Inclusion, HR matters, or Corporate Social Responsibility. We spend at least a third of our time at work or in the office. Companies pay us to be productive, so why would they not invest in our mental wellbeing to make sure we are fit for work?

Admittedly, there is now an increasing trend of workshops and talks on wellbeing, staying healthy, and stress management. "Mindfulness" seems to be the buzz word, as if mindfulness is the solution to everything. I find it a shallow understanding.

'Oh, you have depression. Have you tried mindfulness or meditation?'

If only it was so straightforward! The deeper question is: how do companies' cultures enable or empower employees to speak their minds, share their real emotions, and seek help without stigma or taboo? Even if they are experiencing mental health challenges that aren't work-related?

The Boston Consulting Group and Healthways calculated that US companies could – if they addressed inactivity, stress and alcohol use over a five-year period – save an average of 700 US dollars per year per employee in terms of healthcare costs and productivity[27]. Although these savings are specific to the United States, an increase in productivity can be realised across the world. For example, in a model calculation for 10,000 employees, an intervention cost of 8 US dollars per employee per month would yield an overall ROI potential of 390–755%, depending on location[28].

My company took care of me the best they could. The medical insurance they had for me did not cover psychotherapy, but it did cover antidepressants, other medication and check-ups, which helped immensely. The cost of treatment was perhaps not as comparable as the cost of my being absent from work. I could not physically, mentally, or emotionally perform at work anymore. I lost all the social and cognitive skills I once had – I couldn't even get myself dressed. I would wear the same clothes for days, both to sleep and to mope about in when I was awake. At one point I sat like a statue in the bathtub with my clothes on, ready to take a shower. I stayed there, unmoving, because I had forgotten why I'd got into the bathtub in the first place.

Although I now had the time to do all those things on my bucket list, I had no energy to do so. I couldn't even read the bookshelf of unread books I had accumulated at different airports en route to business trips. The TV flicked on, and I stared at it but saw nothing. It was as though a blank slate of nothingness had clouded my vision.

The mere sight of my company's logo would render me catatonic. I felt so wrong for having thoughts of killing myself. I was burnt out by any contact with people; they seemed to suck away all my energy. This turned into a loathing of others, and I started to avoid them. I ignored calls and would bury my phone under the beanbag chair in the apartment to muffle the ringing. I jumped whenever the phone rang with an unknown number. I did not respond to emails either.

*Delete, delete, delete, delete* ... I deleted half the people I had on my Facebook account, and I restricted access to the rest. I hated seeing the photos of their happy lives, travelling to sunny places like I had done before I became depressed. I wished they would all just leave me alone. I wished they would stop asking me how I was doing, how Beijing was, how life was. Life was shit, if they had to know. And then they would berate me for being ungrateful when I didn't want to answer.

I didn't want to see anyone. I was certain that Timmie was annoyed at the mere sight of me by then – I know I was. I was scared I was becoming a burden, and that he would get sick and tired of me and leave. I hated myself. I was no use to anybody.

I became someone I didn't recognise. Who was this person reflected in the mirror? I used to be calm, collected, and composed. I never cried. I brushed my hair and took care of my skin. I was rational and sensible. I was a strategic planner and executive. Now, my hair had gone limp, my eyes were hollow with dark circles under them, and my complexion was the colour of soil. I hated myself with the utmost passion. Could someone just take me away from this life?

I realised I had had enough. It was time to go.

Timmie had left to go for a drink with his friends, so I could go in peace. I was overtaken by my irrational thoughts and feelings and the meaninglessness of my existence.

So when Timmie came home, he found me slumped, semi-conscious, across the two small steps between my living room and dining room. I could vaguely hear him shuffling, stomping around, and calling someone on the phone, yelling something. Then he picked me up. My head hurt. Did I fall? The last thing I remembered was trying to get a glass of water from the kitchen to wash down the pills.

Timmie dragged my limp body into the elevator, across the cold floor tiles in the lobby, and out onto the driveway. He yelled for the receptionists to hail a cab for us. I was merely a lump of bones shrouded in pyjamas. Where were we going? I was barefoot!

Timmie bundled me into the taxi and I willed my bum to stay on the seat as the driver sped along the dark, empty streets behind Chao Yang Park West Road. In the distance, I heard the chuckles of some *lao wai* (foreigner) heading home after their last drinks. Typical Beijing weekend.

I don't know how long it took to get to the hospital. To me, it felt like an eternity. Timmie picked up my slumped body and carried me from the taxi to the sliding doors of the clinic. He screamed at the security guard for dozing off to sleep and not seeing us approach. A nurse heard us and scrambled to find a wheelchair.

A few nurses scuttled across the room and paged the ER doctor on duty. Gently, they helped me onto the bed. In my daze, I surveyed my sanctuary – it was decorated with white lights and curtains, with white bedsheets and machines that beeped. I even had my own bathroom in this tiny ward. Everything was pristine. There was an eerie peace to it.

I thought I was in heaven, about to meet God. I thought I would have to defend myself as to why I had chosen to die.

I could not stop shivering, even after they put a few blankets over me. Perhaps I was trembling not from the temperature in the room, but from fear – although fear of what, I couldn't say.

One of the nurses (who I later discovered was the head nurse, Dee Dee) stuck a little white instrument softly into my ear. Click. No temperature.

Then they rolled up my pyjama sleeves, wrapped my bony biceps with black elastic tape and stuck a little black ball underneath. They shifted my index finger and put it into a mousetrap-like device and kept it there for a few seconds. *Beep beep beeeeeeep!*

'Pressure 35 / 60,' the nurse noted.

A tall man came into the room – the doctor, I believe. My eyes squinted at the bright ceiling lights, so he ordered for them to be turned off. I heard Timmie mumble something about coming home and finding me on the floor, about not being sure what had happened, and that there was glass everywhere in the kitchen.

Doctor peered into my eyes. 'What is your name?'

'No ... No ... Nochie,' I stammered.

'Do you know what day it is?'

'Umm ... Saturday ... Or the fifth... or Friday?' I managed with gasping breaths.

Doctor felt my head lightly and put his hand on the back of my neck. 'Did that hurt?'

'A little ... I dunno ... I feel so ... so ... um, diiiiiiizzy!' I answered.

There was no lump on my head, so the doctor decided I had not banged it too hard. They ordered an X-ray to see if I had a concussion. I don't even remember passing through the machine.

Later a sudden wave of nausea overcame me and the nurse brought me a basin. I tried to throw up. Water. Spit. Some sort of translucent fluid. The remains of the sleeping pills I'd swallowed had burnt my stomach lining, and I couldn't vomit them back out. I felt even worse.

Timmie went outside with the doctor and I could hear muffled voices behind the curtains. My fate was at their mercy, but I was too exhausted to eavesdrop. They decided that flushing my stomach was not necessary as I was still conscious, but that I had to stay the night for observation. I was deemed to be dehydrated, and obviously drowsy from an overdose of pills.

Nurse Dee Dee came back in with a tray of assorted needles and tape and a few packages of glucose solution. She tied a thick, rubbery band around my arm, and asked me to ball my hand tightly into a fist. My attempt was in vain; my grip was too weak and Timmie had to do it for me. The nurse tapped around my hand and found a relatively chubby blood vessel pounding green beneath the skin. Poke. The needle was in, and she taped it down before connecting the needle to a tube that extended from the packet of glucose. She hung the packet on a stand.

*Dullop, dullop, dollop,* went the IV drip.

I tried to sit up. I thought I had sat up straight, but in fact I was like a sack of potatoes. My eyes flitted open temporarily, but slowly my heavy eyelids clamped down again.

My life flashed before my eyes as I closed them. What had become of me? Was God punishing me for something I had done – or not done?

*Maybe I was a bad person. That's why this is happening to me, I mused. But then I thought, I used to be a strong girl. I can will myself to get better!*

All that time I lay there, half-paralysed and aching with pain, wondering what sort of path of self-destruction I was on. Although my thoughts were muddled by medicine, the bitter irony was that I could now see clearly how I had brought this on myself.

My body needed rest to repair itself. It had sprinted too long without taking a break, giving in to every unreasonable command my mind had given it.

*Finish this excel spreadsheet, even though it's already midnight!*

*Fit in another client meeting!*

*Take the CFA and the GMAT and the LLM exams all in one year!*

*Make more friends!*

*Make your life super perfect!*

Now my body had had enough, and it was rebelling. It was time to reconsider what was more important – the promotion I vied for, or time with my family and friends. Was Harvard Business School my ultimate purpose in life, or should my health take precedence?

The irony of my predicament hit me, for in my ignorance I used to despise those who were depressed. I used to think that life was too precious to waste, and that suicide was stupid. I thought I would never be so low as to contemplate it. Yet the tables had turned. Some mysterious force had flushed my brain of any emotions and interest, and that indifference erased any residual respect I had for life.

Exhaustion flooded me. I could see those who had gone before me beckoning to me, nodding and smiling, and I finally understood why so many people chose to die. I would no longer laugh at them for their choices. Now, I believed that there was a profound wisdom in taking control of one's life and deciding when to relinquish one's last breath – a wisdom that only few would ever comprehend.

When I opened my eyes again, the whole clinic was buzzing and lots of people were bustling around. Timmie was half asleep on the chair next to me. Another doctor came to have one last look at me and decided I could be discharged. I got up feebly to put on my shoes, but then remembered I wasn't wearing any, so the nurse gave me a pair of paper slippers.

Timmie and I got home in a taxi just after lunch. Home – where I hid under the blankets to contemplate what I had done. I was slightly angry I had not succeeded in taking my own life, but I was too drained to devise my next attempt.

Thank goodness I was still on company medical insurance. International hospitals were not cheap! How much was I costing the company to keep me on their books while I was on sick leave, unable to be productive? How much did my medication and trips to the ER cost? Workplace mental health was even less talked about then – eight years ago now – when I was caught in its web. And my company was a responsible one that distributed employee wellbeing surveys to us all every year.

Perhaps at that time, though, I had dismissed stress management training with a haughty attitude. Perhaps I'd seen it as a tool for the feeble, and did not pay attention to the care given to me.

There are still many companies who wave mental health away with a lunchtime yoga class, and many more that have not even put mental wellbeing on the agenda. Countries such as Canada, Australia, the UK and the US are ahead of the curve, understanding that emotional and mental health is just as important – if not more – than physical health. The World Economic Forum and other studies show that it is worth it for companies to invest in their employees' mental health, in order to prevent burnout and depression. Depression screenings yield a 1.7:1 return on investment ratio[29], and there is an average ROI of 3.27 US dollars for every dollar spent on wellness programmes[30]. China and Chinese companies have a lot to catch up on!

My burnout experience was not specific to me. I have since met countless number of people who feel burnt out but do not have the language to express their overbearing sense of weariness. As if a learnt reflex, we blame work for our demise, citing frequent travelling, late nights, unreasonable bosses, flooding workload, and unfair pay. These all exist of course, but they are not the only factors. It is not so clear cut as to say, 'Oh, you are burnt out. It must be your workload!' Work is an easy excuse. Consider cancer: can we really pinpoint the exact cause of why a particular cell in our body started mutating?

With these tangible external forces – such as work or dysfunctional families – on which to focus our complaints, we conveniently forget to look introspectively, and ask ourselves: 'what part am I playing in this?'

How do we cope with these environmental factors? How do we see ourselves in the midst of the environment? How are we burning ourselves out with the choices we make and the reactions we have? Surreptitiously, in the back of our minds, we are convinced of our inadequacies. We have perceived expectations of family, peers, friends, society, expectations, and history. We are wobbled by our insecurities and our commitment to not disappoint. We are more than tired, and have neither the courage to admit it nor the channels through which to vent. We are afraid of the judgment that might befall us if we do.

We are burning ourselves out. I was burnt out from being me, encumbered with achievements, deprived of play, and unable to articulate how I felt.

***Figure 6:*** *Beezie.*
*He is busy running around like no tomorrow but has no idea why. He has no time for life and never slows down. His goal is to do nothing for once, but then he gets so busy that he forgets this.*

# THE JOURNEY

"Everyone has a story if you care to listen. There is no "bad" or "wrong" – our lives, our experiences, our decisions, our feelings, are all part of us."

Enoch Li

# CHAPTER 6

# BRUSH STROKES

'You have severe clinical depression,' proclaimed Dr H.

I blinked. 'When do I go back to work?'

I sank into the black leather couch in Dr H's small office at that first session of psychotherapy. I did not want to be there. Timmie had dragged me to see a doctor, who had then prescribed antidepressants, sent me off for MRI scans, and ordered me to see a psychologist. I dragged my feet the entire way. Psychologists were for loony people, and I was strong enough to cope with whatever stress I had in my life. So why would I need one?

I had seen one a few months ago here in Beijing, when my migraines first started happening. But there were no sparks between us; I felt that she had dismissed me as simply having culture shock. I didn't feel that I needed any counselling or help and was adamant that a month's sick leave would allow me sufficient rest to make the migraines disappear. I would be back at my corner office against floor-to-ceiling glass windows in no time! Wishful thinking indeed. A few months had passed by, the migraines had got worse, and then the depression hit.

Timmie sat down next to me in that first session with this new clinical psychologist. Dr H wanted to know why I was there that day. In a sardonic daze, I told him that I did not want to be there, but Timmie had coerced me into the session. I sat stoically as Timmie explained his observations of my lack of motivation, prolonged time in bed, and general indifference to life. He remarked that the person he saw now was drastically different from the girl he had met a year ago in Tokyo.

Back then, when he first met me, I was strutting around as the gracious hostess of the house party he had crashed. There must have been almost 100 people at the party. People were impressed at how many people I knew from all walks of life. All my friends thought that I had a lot going for me. I was sociable, cheerful, smiley, sparky, and funny. I had the safety of an international expatriate contract for life, youth, energy, intelligence and competence, curiosity for learning, and a heart for helping others. I went to art exhibitions, theatre shows, book clubs, basketball games, and karaoke. I enjoyed myself, sang out of tune, and danced. I was "normal". They all thought I would go far in my career, and maybe champion some sort of cause to make the world a better place.

That had all vanished, completely disappeared without a trace. You would not see any resemblance between that person and the one sitting on the sofa in Dr H's therapy room. I had not combed my hair. Instead I'd shoved it into a pig tail. My clothes were creased and my boots were dusty from my dragging my feet. The circles under my eyes were at their worst. There was no vitality in me, no drive, no interest in anything, and no desire for connection. I was alive in flesh, but dead in mind and spirit.

I avoided eye contact and hugged the cushion for protection as Dr H fumbled through a stack of paper and found the sheet he had prepared. It was a questionnaire of my present preferences and habits in comparison with the fortnight that had just passed. Did I have more, less, or the same appetite as two weeks ago? Did I have more, less or the same sexual drive as two weeks ago? More or less interest in the things I used to enjoy? More or less motivation? More or less contact with friends? Was I still having suicidal thoughts?

I answered "less" for most questions in my hollow voice. I played with my fingers and out of the corner of my eye I saw Dr H jot down my responses. He then scribbled something on the side. He did a quick calculation and gave us his opinion: I had major depression. I was flabbergasted, unable to grasp the verdict. I did not even know what depression meant.

Dr H elaborated on the diagnosis and symptoms, explaining the correlation between stress and mental health. It was more for Timmie's benefit, I thought, for I was still stunned and not paying attention to what he was saying. I could not accept that I was stressed or needed help in any way. I was still strategising my return to work, addressing the blinking red light on my Blackberry and what I would say to my bosses.

Dr H suggested I follow a program of Cognitive Behavioural Therapy, which he would personally administer. It would require seeing him once a week. I was drained and had no interest or motivation in my meagre life by that point, and so I didn't argue. We ended the session with me in a glum mood, but I promised to attend my sessions with Dr H so that Timmie wouldn't have to worry.

Timmie strode out from his office and I dawdled closely behind, head bowed down low. I tried to hide my face in my duck poop green duvet jacket, and if I could, I would have buried my head in the Ugg boots I was wearing. Timmie paid for my session, and we hailed a taxi among the snowdrifts that had concealed Beijing since early November.

It was my first winter in Beijing, months after the first migraine attack. The persistent dryness and the insolent wind made my skin itchy and my eyes hurt. The fear of the harsh winter drove me to stay indoors, even when the sun peeped out for a few hours during the day. Once darkness fell, I became apprehensive and didn't want to be outdoors, lest spirits and shadows engulfed me. I locked myself in, subjecting myself to perpetual suffocation under my blankets. I kept the curtains drawn to block out any demons lurking outside. The sour irony was that I now had more time to sleep than when I was working, but I never felt rested.

Sleeping was a problem that bothered me immensely. Sometimes I slept more than 18 hours a day, in a dilapidated state of semi-consciousness. I would get out of bed and tug my blanket along with me to the sofa. There I would lie down again, staring into nothingness, breaking down into tears. Other times, I would go to bed at night and not be able to fall asleep until dawn arrived. One thing was constant however: I always woke up terrified by nightmares – nightmares of falling through a splitting mountain during a hike. I would choke, wake up, gasp for breath, realise I was just dreaming, and go back to sleep – only to find myself immersed in another frightful scene. In one nightmare a huge butterfly clasped my neck as I tried to flee down a hallway with yellow lights. I swear I felt the weight of its wings on my neck. Even when I took a pair of scissors in the dream and chopped off its wings, I got no relief from the fear.

Most mornings I was wearier than the night before. Perhaps that's because sometimes I would fall asleep at 4:30am, dreaming about the ketchup-coloured beetle car that stalked me as I rode my bike along the suburbs of Perth, Australia. Our family had spent a few years there during my childhood. This had been a recurring dream since I was 7 years old. The fear was so intense I thought the dream was real, and Timmie had to shake me to wake me up.

The migraines had not stopped, and every other day I would be taken over by nausea. I would writhe in agony, my head pulsating.

Dr H asked my regular doctor to prescribe sleeping pills to help me sleep. Good quality sleep was the basic foundation that my body and mind needed to get stronger. That was how I'd tackle the depression.

The combination of sleeping pills and antidepressants sent me into a fuzzy haze. I was drowsy and dizzy, but it was imperative

I took my pills every day. Dr H wanted to make sure my body was given doses of serotonin to bring the chemical imbalances under control. Physiological treatment combined with psychological therapy was my prescription for the time being.

Under Timmie's watch, I attended my psychotherapy sessions without fail. It was the only thing I had on my agenda by then, as I was on sick leave from work. I grew to enjoy the sessions. They gave me a sheltered space to talk, swear, and curse the whole world without fear of reprimands and ignorant comments from friends, who often told me to count my blessings and to stop thinking the way I did. As well as this, Dr H wore bright, lime green shirts!

Despite my initial reticence due to depression, I built a rapport with Dr H. He listened when I mumbled. He asked questions, digging into the depths of my emotions. Sometimes he lectured and I took notes as any diligent student would. He described the cognitive theories of psychology; hidden memories of the psychology classes I used to love found their way back into my conscious mind.

When I could I would ride my bicycle, cutting through the dusty and sandy Beijing wind. The doctor said I needed to exercise, so I tried. Many times I was so fragile that my vertigo kicked in, and I would feel dizzy and fall off my bicycle. I would have to clamber to the curb and wait for Timmie to come and save me.

At a later point I started taking calligraphy classes. 'Relax your wrist,' my calligraphy teacher would instruct me. I was bamboozled. Where was my wrist? I couldn't feel it, not because I didn't know that it hung off the end of my arm. I couldn't feel my body. I was so tense that I couldn't feel any more. I didn't know whether I was tense in my shoulders or back. I didn't know what relaxing meant, because I was used to powering through fatigue.

As I brooded over my depressed self, I had found my teacher by chance. I had always wanted to know more about calligraphy, though of course I didn't have the energy or time when I was in a corporate job. He was a patient teacher and didn't mind even when I had to cancel classes on short notice because I was wrought with another migraine or deep within my depressed bubble. I thought calligraphy might be helpful in learning how to relax and get out of the depression.

Sometimes I was lucky and felt up to it. I would arrive at an unassuming red-brick building where my teacher lived. I would climb four flights of stairs and arrive at an iron gate. I knew it was my teacher's apartment because of the calligraphy he had stuck outside his door, usually a saying about inner peace. I would enter his modest apartment, and immediately a sense of tranquillity would come over me in waves. I'd sit as he made tea. The first few lessons I gulped the tea down, but gradually I learnt to sip and taste the tea. He guided me, telling me to close my eyes and breathe for a few minutes.

Then we would start writing.

He would write one character, and then I would practise. My mind raced wild as I wrote, oblivious to what I was doing or how my body reacted. I was just set on writing the perfect character, a perfect imitation of his. But the harder I tried, the worse the characters looked.

'Focus on the ink at each moment. Not the stroke, not the character. Think about your breath and how it connects with your arm and wrist,' Teacher guided me. I heard him, but I didn't understand.

The desire for perfection was apparent in my calligraphy classes too, for all I wanted was to produce a flawless concoction of ink that looked like a masterpiece. Even with my hobbies I placed too much emphasis on achievement. But the ink on the paper wouldn't transform into legible characters. They were as dispersed as my thoughts and feelings.

During this time I began to self-analyse. I started to think about my behaviour when depressed: lying in bed all day, refusing to eat, not talking to anyone, trying to cut my wrists but being so void of energy that I couldn't break the skin.

I ruminated.

*What is wrong with me? Why am I depressed? What do I even want? Where is my passion?*

*It's futile to keep trying. All work is the same. I got promoted and everyone likes me at work, so maybe I should just be grateful to have a job.*

*I am worthless and no one would miss me.*

*I can't be successful. But what even is success?*

Dr H helped me address these thoughts in therapy. The premise was to equip me with tools to control my thoughts and emotions, before musing over why I was depressed and what had caused it.

My first piece of counselling homework was to probe the thoughts that drove my behaviour and to discover what emotions were behind my self-destructive deeds. Emotions drive thoughts, which determine behaviour. But usually we are blinded by our emotions and we don't understand why we act the way we do.

I was angry. But what was beneath the anger? And why?

Emotions? They were an alien language. I didn't know how I felt underneath that surface layer of anger. My actions were driven by my emotions, but ironically I couldn't articulate what those emotions were. I couldn't say 'I am depressed,' or 'I am disappointed in myself.' I couldn't express my lethargy or loneliness. As a result, I couldn't see that my anal behaviour – filling up my schedules, working too hard – was driven by something deeper than simply the desire to be efficient.

For almost three decades I hadn't known what emotions were there under the surface, let alone find the words for them. Those emotions had been weaned out of me from a young age. I'd had to maintain that strong, accomplished image. I could only be happy, for anything less made me "ungrateful."

I did not know why I cried. I did not know my shoulders were tense. I did not feel myself holding my breath. Everything was disconnected, from my ears to my belly button to my toes. They were like separate beings, existing on their own. My mind was shut out, because the mind did not want to see. I was on autopilot, barely surviving, just sucking air into my lungs. I had no cognition or awareness.

But these emotions were there, all there. I just wasn't aware of them.

And so Dr H guided me and helped me discover my emotions. With his help, I learnt that I had always busied myself because I was full of self-doubt. I felt distraught and unworthy. And concealed underneath my anger were feelings of pain, heartache, loneliness, disappointment, alienation and humiliation.

Dr H helped me to dig out all the thoughts swirling in my little brain, those that were driven by my emotions. He said that my thoughts were irrational because they were not logical, or were based on false assumptions. What makes these ideas irrational, or maladaptive, is the belief that they are always correct. Sure, working hard will increase your chances for success, but success is not guaranteed. There are times when we do everything right, and we still do not get what we want. For some people, this leads to the conclusion that they are lazy, no good, incompetent, or weak, resulting in loss of self-esteem. Sometimes it leads to depression.

Common thinking traps include "jumping to conclusions", where one overestimates the likelihood of negative events happening. One interprets things negatively when there is little or no evidence to support that interpretation and ignores evidence that suggest a more likely outcome. "Thinking the worst" or "catastrophising" is where one automatically predicts that the worst possible scenario is going to happen, without considering other possible outcomes.

I did both to zealous perfection. Now that I think about it, some of my catastrophising was amusing, to say the least. But it felt so real that I believed in my catastrophic thoughts with blind faith.

I recounted a childhood memory. In it, a big hairy dog chased me down a dark alleyway. I could hear the dog bark, and it sounded like it was right behind me. But in reality, the dog was chained up. Every adult who was present at the time laughed at me, but to my five-year-old self, it was a traumatic. Since then I had been scared of dogs, and every time I saw one I would expect it to bite me or go crazy all of a sudden. Dr H helped me evaluate these automatic thoughts.

- *Do I know for certain that X will happen?*
- *What evidence do I have for this fear or belief?*
- *What do I think happened in that situation?*
- *Could there be other explanations?*
- *What is the worst that could happen? How bad is that? Have I been able to cope with similar situations in the past?*
- *Even if what I think might happen happens, can I live through it?*

The point was to create healthier thought patterns. As I gained more understanding of the world, I came to know that not all dogs bite, and I just need to walk calmly by.

As I went about the self-analysis, I would feel better – and then crash harder. My mind went up and down, up and down, up and down. I would crash, defragment, try to drown myself, try to overdose on pills, and then slowly glue the pieces back together. Recovery was not a straight, upwards line on a chart.

As the antidepressants started to take effect and I gained a little more energy, I was able to put my compulsion to self-harm into action. Before, in my acute lethargic state, I hadn't even been able to lift a finger.

My fluctuations in mood became extreme. I was digging deeper and wider into the space of self-awareness.

Most times Dr H challenged me to look at myself. It was hard work. Often it was too confronting for my psyche to bear, and I would break down again. Emotions were a completely new domain to me.

Not all emotions feel pleasant. Some of them take us to dark places. But if we can focus on our negative feelings and identify them – in the same way I have learnt to focus on the split moment that my ink touches the bamboo paper, the strength of the lightness, and the

**Figure 7:** *Peace with Ease*

synchronisation of every breath with my wrist movements – then we can find an inner emotional awareness.

Emotional awareness is to allow oneself to fully experience emotions as they happen – and accept them. There are no positive or negative, good or bad, or right or wrong emotions. They are simply emotions, a message to us.

I saw with calligraphy that, if I was present in the moment, the final character appeared in its own time, with all its blemishes and uniqueness.

**Figure 8:** *Slurpie.*
*Slurpie is a bit lopsided. He's an outcast and is always on his own, but he goes about his way, just being himself.*

# CHAPTER 7

# FLOPPIE

Floppie saved my life.

One day I was huddled in the foetal position on my bed, curtains drawn, buried in my sheets. I was a lump of misery. I spent most of my depressed days in bed or on the living room floor in downtown Beijing. I had lost all my energy and I sobbed impulsively. It seemed natural that after reaching my summit in Tokyo, the logical step was to come down. I just didn't expect to fall this far down. In my mind, the stretch of nothingness was omniscient. There was one dim street lamp in that darkness, but however I crawled towards it, it did not come closer. There was no hope left in my mind. Floppie stood by me on the floor. He looked at me kindly, gave me a pat on the head, and smiled gently as if to say, 'I will be here, whatever befalls you.'

Floppie was a stuffed toy bear.

I had locked myself in at home for some weeks already since being given sick leave, unable to face the outside world or look at my rugged self in the mirror. Apart from the regular psychotherapy sessions and calligraphy classes, I would not leave the apartment, sometimes not even my bed.

On a pivotal winter day in January 2010 – the weather being fit for my depressed mood – Timmie somehow managed to drag me out of bed to go for a walk to the nearby mall. I had no interest, but I was too tired to protest. I dragged my feet and kept my head to the ground as I walked. Chance had it that at some point Timmie had to go to the bathroom, so I loitered at the shop nearby to wait for him. There in the shop window I saw a soft toy bear! It looked so soft. It just sat there looking up at me, giving me a little smile. I smiled back. When Timmie came into the shop to look for me, he saw a faint smile on my face for the first time in many weeks. He bought the bear for me.

Timmie asked me to give the bear a name. Without thinking twice, I named the him Floppie.

A few days later Timmie wanted me to go out for a walk again. When I refused, he suggested, 'How about we take Floppie to play in the snow?' I lit up and agreed. We went to the Forbidden City moat, which was covered in pristine snow. Timmie put Floppie down and said we should take some photos with him. I giggled, and for a while I was distracted from any negative or

*Figure 9: Floppie in the snow.*

suicidal thoughts. I just played and enjoyed the time. I decided it was too cold and gave Floppie a hat and vest to wear.

'Why name him Floppie?' Timmie asked me.

'Because he just flops around all day. He's tired and sad all the time,' I answered.

'Oh, and he eats mosquitoes,' I added as an afterthought.

At the age of 30, I was playing with a stuffed toy bear.

Many would see this as childish – and so did I. I was ashamed and embarrassed to admit I had stuffed toy animals, and that I *talked* to Floppie, played with him, went sightseeing with him in the midst of Beijing's snowy winter.

Floppie was from a brand called Gund, and this particular line of bears was named "Snuffles". Since Floppie, this bear collection had grown into a full-on Beardom (Bear Kingdom). The bears were the same design, but different colours or sizes. I gave each new arrival a name and a personality. They gave me a reason to socialise again. When isolation kicked in as a depressive symptom, playing with bears became an antidote. It got me out of the apartment. In my indolent phase I started a photo blog for the bears to showcase their travels as I had once done. I made up short stories for them.

At that time, I had no idea that with the bears, I had created a safe space for myself. There I could rediscover my creativity and heal. I did it because it made me happy and distracted me from ruminating, from the negativity in my head. Timmie called this indulgence Bearapy – bear therapy. I became the Bearalist – the Bear Specialist.

Some of these bears were my "old self", or an image of myself that I had internalised. Take for instance Fuzzie the banker bear, who is very calculating and only helps people in return for favours. He reminded me of my corporate days, of the scepticism I held towards people, and how I may have treated others. It was difficult to see that I may have been insincere in some relationships, especially at the workplace. And yet it was also part of me that I needed to accept and embrace, because I am not a saint. By projecting this part of myself that I didn't like onto an unassuming, cute-looking, stuffed toy bear, looking at myself became more tolerable.

I have a talent for seeing the worst in every situation and assessing all the worst-case scenarios. Sometimes I tend to blame it on studying law and learning about credit and risk assessment in my finance career. Whenever others marvelled at how their sparkly glasses were half full, I would critique them, noticing how empty, dirty and broken they were. Such was my modus operandi. Many have told me that I need to change this. I am not sure. It is not good or bad, and I would rather acknowledge that this attitude is part of me. And now that I have identified it, I can entertain other perspectives without feeling that I have to change myself, or that my mindset is defective. It is simply different.

**Figure 10:** *Chillie sailing on Sydney Harbour.*

And so entered Shinie and Happie bears. Shinie, the bear who sees the positives in every situation, and Happie, who is simply joyful and grateful for being alive, serve as reminders that not all negative thoughts are realities, and that the conclusions must be tested.

Part of my burning out was because I hadn't given myself time to breathe or take a break. This is very much like Beezie, the busy bear who cannot control his impulses to run around and do things. On the contrary, I now look to emulate Chillie, a bear whose goal in life is to enjoy himself and chillax, without feeling guilty about wasting time. Beezie and Chillie find each other incomprehensible and go about their own lives – though perhaps they have left some influence on each other. Perhaps they're both a reminder for me to take a pause every now and then?

When I found life hard, Punkie would remind me that I could have fun and play harmless tricks on others. Gourmie would bring me some Bearchelin-starred chicken wings as snacks, and that day would be fun again. Snobbie is self-righteous and has

**Figure 11:** *Lining up for bear hugs.*

delusions of grandeur, believing that he is always right, whereas Dummie bear understands that some bears don't have the same opportunities as others. He knows that other bears are not stupid.

With these bears, I was able to explore my inner thoughts and emotions, and probe into my fears and shadows. I was *playing* again.

During childhood, we all play. The first few years of our lives, we existed in our own worlds as children, not caring what other people thought. We played as we wanted to, and even ate mud if we wanted to, testing our environments. Some of us had an object we would keep close at all times, be it a toy or a blanket. Then, as we moved into adulthood, our ability to play dwindled as we undertook more activities regarded as "productive". The importance of objects and toys in our learning and development processes diminished, and they were labelled as "childish." We learnt judgment when adults told us to do something or refrain from other actions. We learnt "right" from "wrong". From then on – similar to most people in the corporate world these days – the rest of my life was spent doing what was considered "good" to society. I wanted to live up to others' expectations. I conjured up an image of what I wanted to achieve, one that would guarantee success, popularity, love, admiration and respect. I cared too much what others thought of me, how they valued me, and what they said about my behaviour.

Playing was the process that enabled me to see myself again and taught me not to hate myself. In the playing space, I set myself free from depression. Playing served as a source of entertainment and amusement. When I had nightmares and couldn't sleep, Timmie would tell me to visualise the bears on a train journey or in a restaurant and ask me what they might be doing. I would drift into sleep, chuckling at the mischief the bears conjured up. This free association and imagination distracted me from stressful times. My study room was dubbed The

Bear Room, a haven that housed my favourite things such as the bears, jigsaw puzzles, and books. It is a happy place, a place for comfort, solace, and safety. I would run into the room after a nightmare or an argument with Timmie, and then I would feel okay. Sensory play dissipated my anxiety.

This was the miracle. Play was part of my life once again. It was a long-lost skill that I had either suppressed, forgotten, or despised. Perhaps the fact that I was not playing had brought me to my demise. I had discarded play, the very thing that was vital to wellbeing. But play hadn't forsaken me.

When we bring playfulness into the forefront of our minds again, we can engage in it consciously, and give

*Figure 12: Bears with Bamboo, the dog.*

ourselves a dose of playfulness a day. I was afraid I would be ridiculed. But the more I did it, the less embarrassed I felt, and the more I accepted that this was me – I just wanted to play.

Today, years later, all my friends know of the bears and ask about them. I started travelling around the world with a different bear each time. Sometimes I took them to events in Beijing. When I travelled with my bears, I engaged in specific play. I was thinking of stories to create for them. I looked at the world through their eyes, through the different personalities I possessed. I created scenarios in my imagination and played out interactions between the bears. I thought about how they would react to the same situation, what they did when they travelled. It was part illusion, part reality, for all the bears were facets of myself – who I was, who I am, who I will be. These activities were creative, fun, and a cushioned way for me to come to terms with my lack of omnipotence and omniscience.

With these teddies I was able to see myself clearly in the mirror. I split off the bits I didn't like about myself and put them into toy bears. I played, created stories, saw the world through their eyes, analysed myself, and confronted my shadows. I faced what I disliked about myself. It is not so much about discarding the so-called "bad" bits of myself. Instead I now embrace these bits of me that I don't like. I merged my ideal self with my real self. It is not the glitzy picture most would like to see, but it is real. So, why shy away from the realness?

The most important step was to reintegrate those parts and understand that they are all me. All these different bears were myriad facets of who I was, making me the unique individual. Putting life into play mode, I realised that I didn't have to be so hard on myself or take perceived mistakes so seriously. There was no "bad" or "wrong" – my life, my experience, my decisions, were all part of me.

I found Floppie by chance, and he found me. Play happened by chance. It was only because I was engulfed in my bubble of gloom, not caring anymore about my image, that I gave play another chance. I hugged Floppie tightly when scared. I flooded his soft fur with tears. He distracted me from depression when I was taking photos of him. By projecting myself onto a toy bear, I came to know myself. I opened up to what I did not know I did not know. Through Floppie's lethargy, I saw my lifeless mind and soul.

I had lived for others and suppressed my inner child.

I had strived for an image of external success, and then lost myself.

I was rewarded with daily migraines, burnout, and a debilitating clinical depression that lasted for a few years.

Until depression brought playfulness back to my life.

You have seen throughout the book the different bears and their personalities. For more bears and their personalities, visit The Bearchive at http://bearapy.me/bearchive/ and also see the blog at http://bearapy.me.

**Figure 13:** Floppie.
*Floppie is always sleepy. He watches TV when he's awake and eats mossies (mosquitoes). He's always there for me with a smile.*

# CHAPTER 8

# HUGS

During my worst days, I could not control my sobbing or hatred for the world. I despised myself for being in this deplorable state of being; breathing but dead. I wouldn't have walked out of this zombie state if not for people around to support me, in particular Timmie, who was my boyfriend at the time and is now my husband.

I hallucinated, haunted by a man in a black cape. I shrieked when I saw him. He would stand there in the shadows, watching me from under his dark hood. The shadows concealed his body, but I could make out the shape of a black cape. His eyes were piercing, his gaze intense. He perused me, scanning my thoughts, digging them out from deep inside my brain. The man did not move and he never looked away. I was scared that I was becoming delusional because Timmie couldn't see him.

On one occasion I buried my head into the cushions on the sofa and screamed. Timmie came running out to me and embraced me. I lifted my head a tiny inch and saw that the man was still there in the same place, in the same pose. He wouldn't leave me. He wouldn't let me go free. He never talked to me, so I didn't know what he wanted. He never approached me either.

Had he come to take me away? Or was he there to reprimand me?

I yelled again and started whimpering. Timmie held me tighter, quietly laying down next to me and holding my hand. That was all he did.

I thought I was going mad. The black man in the black cape only showed up when no one could see him, when only Timmie could see me shudder and curl up into a trembling ball.

This was not me. I was not me.

*Would someone please deliver me from this evil?* I thought.

I was sure I was going crazy. I saw Elijah waiting for me outside my window with his chariots of fire. I saw Angel Gabriel, who sat by my bathtub, waiting for me to go to heaven with him. I was already in heaven, for Enoch in the Bible was someone who walked with God for 300 years. God took him to heaven without him experiencing death. Perhaps it was my fate to experience the physical death that the original Enoch had not.

It must have been torture for Timmie, to see me like this every day, wanting to rot away. I was unlike the person he had fallen in love with. I acted strange, was cranky at everything, and refused to do anything.

One weekend, before I'd been diagnosed with depression, I decided I wanted to go to Qingdao – a coastal city north of Beijing – to chill out for a weekend. I made the decision on a whim, and it alerted to Timmie that something wasn't right, because normally I would plan trips way ahead of time. I wanted to go alone at first, but Timmie insisted on coming with me. I thought it would be special to spend some time together after the move from Tokyo to Beijing, as I had been caught up with work. He shares his first-hand account[31]:

*I had a bad feeling about the whole thing. It didn't seem right. It was too sudden, not like her. I was afraid Nochie wanted to kill herself. I was afraid she'd think this was the last weekend away we would have. I thought she wanted to do one last special thing before she died – something to make her smile. I didn't know what to do or who to call.*

*I eventually called an emergency hotline run by the clinic she was going to for her migraines. I explained that I thought my girlfriend wanted to take her own life, so I was put through to a psychologist. I can't remember much about what he said, except that I had to keep a solid watch over Nochie and not let her be alone. Without any proof of her harming herself, there wasn't much they could do.*

*I wondered whether or not to go to Qingdao. Maybe I could have invented an excuse as to why we shouldn't go. But then I figured that if Nochie really wanted her life to end, she would jump out of her office building and I wouldn't be able to stop her.*

*This was the first major incident where I was worried enough to call and ask for help with what to do.*

Friends and family wanted to help but didn't know how. They were trying to reason with someone who couldn't see reason in anything. My pet peeve would be when someone said to me, 'I just want to know that you are doing okay.' What drove me nuts was the phrase "I just want to know ...", which suggested that the priority was how good a job they were doing as friends. They wanted to know I was smiling, to convince themselves that their worlds were still full of sunshine. They wanted to know how I was doing so they could feel good about themselves. It was about them, not me.

In the beginning of my depression, Timmie attempted all logic and reasoning with me, trying to show me that depression was not the end of the world. He too wanted to know that I was "fine" before he went to work, so he could have some sort of peace of mind until he came home at the end of the day. I rejected his efforts and looked at him with hollow eyes. He became exasperated, especially at my constant pleas for death:

*The effect on my daily life was the biggest impact and was definitely a challenge. Nochie would burst into tears and have severe mood swings that I did not know how to deal with. I tried to say the right things, but it hardly ever helped. Then I would get frustrated and sometimes lose my temper and become angry. I am generally a positive person, but sometimes it was hard to stay so. I would get up and be excited about the day, but she just wanted to die – this was a very difficult concept for me to reconcile.*

*Overall, I felt frustrated. There really wasn't anything I could say that would help the situation. I just had to be there for her. When the therapist first said that Nochie would need a year of treatment, I thought that was way too long and an exaggeration. In the end, it took more than a few years before she was herself again.*

*The migraines and associated physical illnesses also made it difficult for me. Sometimes I would have to leave work or a party and rush home to take care of her. One time I came home and found her semi-conscious at the bottom of the staircase. I didn't know if she had fallen or hit her head, so I had to carry her to a taxi and go to the hospital.*

*Another thing that proved to be extremely hard for me to do was to put Nochie's needs first. So even if I was at an amazing party having the time of my life, if Nochie called and needed me I had to leave immediately without even saying goodbye to my friends. This took a bit of time to get used to without feeling resentful, but once accustomed to it I felt a sense of responsibility I had never felt before and it helped me grow up.*

Gradually, and with the help of my psychotherapist, Timmie came to understand that what he saw as illogical was the most logical to my mind. So, instead of trying to convince me to see his point of view, he learnt to overcome his line of reasoning and come to my side of the world. He could not understand what I felt, but he did not negate it. He stopped making sure I was "alright" – unlike many others, who simply wanted to ensure that they would not have to go through the torment of grieving my potential self-inflicted death. Timmie stopped fighting me, and instead accompanied me in my emotional roller coaster. He simply said, "I know," when I told him that the act of breathing was a torment.

I couldn't have carried on without Timmie by my side to keep me alive. My migraines debilitated me, and when they hit, they hit *hard*. If Timmie was out during that time – even though rationally I knew that him coming home was not going to make the migraine go away – I called him. I depended on him, needed reassurance that he had not forsaken me. Back in those days, he liked going out. And so having to suddenly drop everything to come home because I was in physical pain or in an extreme mood and talking gibberish on the phone was frustrating for him, to say the least.

Timmie's love for me was immense. He put me before himself and his wants. He put my needs before his demands to know that I would get better. It was about me, not him.

I had a few close friends who tolerated my self-loathing during those few years. And I had lost friends because of the depression. I also distanced myself from those critical of my experience because I did not need to add in extra guilt and shame, as if depression was a result of my wrongdoing – I felt guilty and ashamed enough as it was. Most people who heard I had depression or such severe migraines wanted to help. I received a flurry of suggestions as to which doctor or what alternative medicine to try. I appreciated those suggestions, and at the same time, they became a burden, for it made me more conscious of the fact that I did not seem to be getting any better. Most people were losing patience with me. Going to see a different doctor itself took energy, and I did not have much then. People suggested Reiki, traditional Chinese medicine, acupuncture, meditation, yoga, chiropractors, dieticians, brain specialists, neurologists, qi gōng … I was getting desperate, and I felt apologetic whenever someone offered options or things I could do. Even though I was pressured by their advice, I still felt I was obliged to be grateful – they only wanted to help.

For someone who hasn't been through depression, any powerful imagination cannot come close to knowing what it feels like. Anyone going through depression cannot explain it, for anything other than breathing by reflex takes immense effort. Over time I came to understand the rift between those who want to help but don't know how, and those who have good intentions but make the depressed even more desolate. Many say things off the top of their heads, forgetting that depression is nothing like "usual".

Having been on both sides, I wanted to clear things up. I came up with this list of things to avoid saying to a depressed person. This list was first published on my blog, NochNoch.com. It has gathered over 1,000 comments and is by far the most read post of my entire blog's survival[32]. I republished it last year on Thrive Global, and every week I see that the article gets widely read. This looks good statistically, and is encouraging that people are looking for advice to help those around them – but it also points to the painstaking fact that there must be so many out there fighting through depression every moment. They need our help.

Help needs to come in the form of what that person needs, not what we think they need. So, here is what I suggest *not to* say to a depressed person:

## 1. 'Remain positive.'

**I think:** *Duh! I know – but how? To me, my reality is that the world has already caved in. What is irrational to you makes utmost sense to me. I am so angry / upset / sad / lonely / devastated / hopeless / in despair ... Why can you not understand me?*

**I feel:** Like I want to recoil further into my shell, to avoid future contact and meaningless advice. You never told me how to remain positive.

## 2. 'Don't think like that.'

**I think:** *Why not? What is wrong with thinking like I do? It is an honest opinion. I really think this. It is negative all right, but*

95

*that's what I think, so what is wrong? How should I think instead? Like you? But I do not agree with you. Will I become you if I think like you?*

**I feel:** I did something wrong for thinking a certain way, and you reprimanded me for thinking so. Thus, I withdraw, and berate myself for thinking the way I do, and spiral further down into depression due to self-criticism.

### 3. 'Pull yourself together' / 'Snap out of it' etc.

**I think:** *How? Snap out of what? I don't want to be like this either. Do you think it's fun?*

**I feel:** Completely useless and hopeless, that I am incapable of holding myself together and getting better. Depression snowballs when you feel this incompetent.

### 4. 'Why do you need to be depressed?'

**I think:** *I wish I knew. Doctors said it is something to do with my serotonin levels. I do not know. I do not know. I DO NOT KNOW!*

**I feel:** Accused of committing a heinous crime. Confused, because I don't know what happened to make me depressed and how it all happened. Lost, since I don't know how to get out of depression. I feel inferior and bad about myself, so I hide from you as well because I don't want to feel inadequate.

### 5. 'Look at how lucky you are already! Be thankful!'

**I think:** *I am thankful for what I have. But what does that have to do with depression? Doctors and every website I have read say depression is an illness. Depression needs to be treated as any other sickness. You are lucky too, be thankful – stop having a freaking cold! Stop sneezing germs into the air I breathe!*

**I feel:** Misunderstood, perceived as a spoilt, ungrateful little girl when I am not. I feel frustrated for being misunderstood, so I cry, wail, and feel sad. I retreat into my hiding place – again.

### 6. 'Go and do something, and you will feel better.'

**I think:** *Go and do what? I can't be bothered. I'm tired. I'm not interested. I have no energy. I just want to sleep. Doing something will not make me feel better. Leave me alone.*

**I feel:** Tired and lethargic, with no energy to even think about what to do. Harassed, because you keep telling me to do something.

### 7. 'What is wrong with you?'

**I think:** *I WISH I KNEW. I wish I knew. Oh, how I wish I knew. Can you tell me? Can somebody tell me? I don't want to be like this. Why am I like this?*

**I feel:** Absolutely hopeless, because I don't know why I became like this. I'm unable to find out the reasons behind my depression. I feel belittled and angry at myself. I cannot deal with this. I might as well die.

### 8. 'You should do this ...' or 'You should not do this ...' (such as kill yourself).

**I think:** *Why? This is my life; I am allowed to end it if I want.*

*Why should I eat? I'm not hungry.*

**I feel:** Patronised by your condescending tone (even if you did not have one). Rejected for not doing what you think I am supposed to do. It's another bash at my already dwindling self-confidence – you just succeeded in making me feel more desperate and more depressed.

### 9. 'There are people worse off than you – be grateful for what you have!'

**I think:** *But you told me not to compare myself to others when I told you I was envious of those who have achieved more than me. It's hypocritical if I'm therefore allowed to compare myself to those less fortunate than myself! I know you're trying to tell me to count my blessings – I do. Trust me, I do. But how does this solve* *my depression? I still feel that life is not worth living, despite being grateful for what I have. I am too tired to carry on and try.*

**I feel:** Baffled as to why sometimes you tell me not to compare myself to others, and yet other times you tell me I should. I don't understand how being thankful makes me feel better, because what I have now has no meaning and no value to me. I JUST WANT TO DIE. Maybe if I died, there'd be more food for those who don't have any.

Proceed to jumping out the window from the 30th floor.

### 10. 'It's all in your head …'

**I think:** *I know. But how do I change my head? It's not my fault. I didn't want this. I cannot control it. I am trying, but I can't!*

**I feel:** Furious at myself for not being able to control my thinking. Inept at everything I am trying to do and worse, for disappointing you. Alone, because no one can understand me, so I alienate myself. I feel that I'm doomed to fail and I might as well die.

It was painful to see so many comments from readers on this blog post, sharing what didn't help them either, or what drove them further into their depression. It is a tricky line to tread for family and friends of depressed people, for what sounds like something helpful could unintentionally send their loved ones over the edge. We, the depressed, do not make it easy for the people around us, given the complex mishmash of emotions we experience.

There were some things that Timmie and my close friends said or did that I found helpful, which I again first posted on my blog. These words and gestures reassured me that I was loved, and helped me to continue on my recovery journey[33]:

**What I suggest to do in order to help a depressed person:**

**1. Tell them, 'I am here for you, whenever you want.'**

I felt like I had someone to hold on to, even though I had no strength or desire to talk to anyone.

**2. Tell them, 'Hey! Did you see the latest app / see the funny video about xyz?'**

Instead of asking 'How are you?' (to which the response would inevitably be 'shit!' from me), one of my friends simply sent me a message every day to talk about irrelevant topics. Modern technology definitely made it easy and inexpensive. Even though this had nothing to do with my health or depression, these quips distracted me from my consistent bouts of crying and made me want to poke my head out from under the covers.

**3. Just lie with them when they cry.**

Timmie would just lay beside me when I was on the living room floor crying. He brought me tissues and hugged me. He didn't ask me why. Neither did he simply tell me not to cry. He just sat there with me. When got tired from crying and fell asleep, I would wake up and feel a small amount of release and comfort.

**4. Tell them, 'I can't necessarily agree with – or understand – how you feel, but I respect that these are your emotions and it's your perspective.'**

My thoughts were undoubtedly irrational. I lamented about life and complained about every menial aspect of it. I had no confidence in myself, despite my so-called achievements. I was hopeless. Every day, I would tell Timmie that I saw no point in living, that I hated myself, and that I would prefer to rot at home instead of going to do some exercise. In the beginning he tried to reason with me, and told me how living could be meaningful, how I could help others, and how my worries were exaggerated. He tried to tell me that I had a blessed life and many things for which to be thankful, but I had a counterargument for every point he raised. It deflated him, which made me feel worse.

Eventually he realised that, when I was spiralling in my thoughts, reasoning with me was not going to help. I was not looking for a debate. What I needed was empathy – or, at least, sympathy – and reassurance that it was fine to feel the way I felt. It was key that I could embrace my emotions and not feel guilty for feeling them. Only by acknowledging my feelings could I then decipher the thoughts behind them and find ways to cope.

## 5. Tell them you believe that they are seeing what they're seeing.

No one could see the black-caped man who was following me. The temptation for anyone not suffering from a mental health problem is to dismiss the person and tell him or her that what they see is not real. Whether their visions are real or not isn't the point. Trying to get me to question my visions made me feel worse about myself. When Timmie affirmed my belief, even though he couldn't see what I saw, it told me that I had his unconditional love, and that I could trust him to not ridicule me. It helped me talk about what was going through my head. Only through opening up could I get better.

## 6. Ask them, 'Can I do anything for you? Do you want some water? Honey lemon? Soup? Chicken wings?'

Usually my response was 'No.' Nevertheless, it made me feel cared for. On rare occasions it stirred my appetite and I would munch on something. It meant a lot, when you consider that I had lost all interest in food and had lost about 10kg in weight over this period. I did not have enough nutrition in my body, and therefore no vigour to do anything. Getting me to eat was an achievement, which steered me towards getting stronger.

## 7. Ask them if they want to do something that brings them comfort.

When Timmie suggested going to the park or taking pictures in the snow, it sparked some motivation within me. I threw on some old clothes (with jeans that didn't match) and scrunched up my limp hair to go outdoors for a while. Going out then added to the chain effect and, combined with the little things above, encouraged me to open up and seek help.

## 8. Offer to accompany them to appointments.

It might be that the depressed person needs the help and company of others in order to go to their therapy sessions. My denial period was longer than the Great Wall of China. Even when Dr H told me, 'You are severely depressed and need to be put on antidepressants', I refused to acknowledge that there was a problem, and so I didn't seek to resolve it. When I couldn't admit that I was stressed or depressed and refused to go to see a psychologist, Timmie would physically drag me out the door and into a taxi. He'd escort me to Dr H's office – and he would make sure I stayed there. He also made sure I took my medication every day.

## 9. Say nothing.

Most of the time, not saying anything was the best thing for my friends to do. I just needed a brain dump, someone to listen without judging me or recommending solutions. I just needed to know that someone was there and would not make me feel guilty for feeling bad about myself.

## 10. Give them a hug.

Just a cuddle, a bear hug. Sit next to them for a while. I found it so soothing – it really calmed me down and made me feel loved, even though I was basking in self-hatred.

## 11. Respect the distance.

I hid from the world for months on end. I got so agitated when calls were long and seemed never-ending. I was scared of people at one point, and I needed the distance to be with myself. When I needed space, I needed space.

It was a more than miracle for Timmie to have stuck with me through it all. Even if I had lost everything else to depression, I gained a husband. It must have been true love!

Timmie, again:

> When she was crying, when she couldn't sleep and when wanted to die, it was useless for me to tell her that everything would be okay and that life was worth living. She just could not see my point. Instead, I learnt to distract her with made-up stories and massages.
>
> It was sometimes easy to feel resentful of the fact that Nochie and I were on totally different wavelengths. But I just kept saying to myself, 'Let's give it one more month and see how she is', and I managed to get through. I was confident that it was a temporary situation. I had known Nochie for a year and a half before the depression, and she was such an amazing person. I knew that with time she could get back to that point. I was convinced the depression would make her stronger.
>
> We had just moved countries to live together and were therefore in a committed relationship. I think if it had been a less serious relationship, I might not have been able to stick through it.

I know I was difficult in the best of times. In the worst of times, I cannot even begin to imagine. My wailing was endless, but Timmie would just lay there with me through it all. I felt soothed by his presence. If not for Timmie, I would not be typing this right now. He kept me alive.

One time, he played me the song 'Chasing Cars' by Snow Patrol. Holding me on his lap, he stroked my hair and said, 'We'll just forget the world ... it will be okay, Nochie. It will be okay.'

**Figure 14:** *Biggie.*
*His sheer size makes him feel awkward and shy, but he has lots of love and bear hugs to give.*

# THE MAGIC

**"Adults are just outdated children"**

**Dr Seuss**[34]

# CHAPTER 9

# BEARAPY

What is the one toy you have kept with you all these years? What is that one toy that moves with you or stays next to your bed? It might be one of the squeaky plastic ones that are shockingly noisy and (in my view) irrelevant to a child's development. Maybe it's a scrap piece of paper, a coin, a tin lid, a toothpick model – even a sock. Mine were Lucky Trolls, dutifully packed in storage in Hong Kong. I've since replaced them with 40 stuffed toy bears, and they sit among Dr Seuss books, Jimmy's illustration books[35], candles, poo toys, and other rickety racketies.

Objects have a long history. We are surrounded by them. They are dear to us, carrying sentimental value. But to some people, they might seem strange – why would we keep a match box next to our pillow when the matches have been burnt? These people have also lost their imagination.

But for wide-eyed children, the matches can be a doorway to a world that only they can see. In my imagination, marshmallows grow on trees and fishes in the lakes deliver lollipops. Occasionally, it rains soda pop. My friends are called Pipsqueak, Rodent, and Muddie.

Imagination has opened up my mind. When I lost my playfulness I lost my inspiration. It shut down my soul.

My life-saving experience with objects and toys, coupled with the psychology of playfulness, became the premise behind my social entrepreneurial business venture, Bearapy. The term was coined by Timmie, and in the beginning it was simply the name given to the photoblog that displayed my adventures and stories about my bears. Today it has evolved into an organisation, with the mission of making the world mentally healthy by using play to help those who are stressed, burnt out, and depressed.

Bearapy has also set a course for companies and organisations interested in employees' wellbeing. It uses the innovative approach of playfulness and personalising workspaces with objects. Through workshops, talks, and online programmes, Bearapy raises awareness of mental health and also does pro bono work for support groups.

Bearapy's development started with my depression and the instinctual naming of Floppie. The progression took place during my organisational psychology studies at a business school after I had emerged from the depression. I was looking for my next career, a new professional identity. One of my professors then suggested that I write a case paper on the bears. I thought he was out of his mind – but then I entertained the idea and did so. In writing the case and reading the psychological research on objects, I figured out the significance of Floppie and all the other bears' names and personalities.

All the bears were different facets of me, although when I started talking to my bears years ago, I didn't understand that I was projecting myself onto them. Floppie was reminiscent of my days spent flopped on the couch and not doing much else aside from watching television and sleeping. Then there was Fuzzie, the banker bear who calculated every single cent and busied himself only with money and status, an image of myself that I loathed for a long time. However, in a story I made up about Fuzzie – in which he finds a bargain during a bulk purchase of plasters – this bear persona became more amusing than threatening.

Projection is a defence mechanism, an unconscious psychological way to help us reduce anxiety induced by potentially harmful stimuli. The most common defence mechanism is denial – proclaiming 'I am not drunk!' after a long night out, for example. But projection as a defence mechanism takes unpleasant feelings and casts them onto others.

Take, for instance, the drunk person. Instead of admitting that they're hungover when they wake up, they'll talk to their dog like he or she is the hungover one – 'I bet you're feeling a bit rough this morning, aren't you!' In this way, they are protected from feeling bad about themselves.

This process happens in your unconscious, but we can become aware of it. When we use projection in the process of playing, we are expressing the feelings that we might not understand or can't articulate. Often, we unconsciously project these feelings, emotions, and personalities onto inanimate objects[36]. Psychoanalysts have long studied our relationship with objects (although many of these studies sadly remain in academic journals).

If you think about your daily lives, you will see that you use objects in many ways. When travelling, many people take comfortable objects that are familiar to them to keep in hotel rooms. Some even rearrange temporary places like hotel rooms or office cubicles into settings similar to their cosy homes. People become attached to things like stuffed toy animals, figurines or (regrettably) mobile phones, and we may become agitated or stressed without them[37]. In playing, however, we can use projection on these external objects for introspection[38]. The objects give us distance from the unpleasant feelings, or the bits of ourselves we do not wish to embrace.

This kind of personalised play is a safety net that allows us room to be creative and imagine new possibilities. In psychology-speak, the objects could be termed "transitional". The term was coined by Donald Winnicott in his book, *Playing and Reality*. He studied children and saw that many of them had a toy (like a teddy bear or safety blanket) that they would carry around with them. He called these "transitional objects" because children were learning about the world. The object, as a constant in their lives, helped the children to understand the difference between reality and their imagination, to make sense of their environments, and to find independence and autonomy in the growing up process[39]. Applied to adults, these objects were coping mechanisms for anxiety and emotional trauma.

Sigmund Freud used the term "cathexis"[40] to describe emotional attachment to tangible objects. Simply put, objects incite emotions, feelings, and thoughts in us. Winnicott took it further, explaining how adults relate to objects: "The object has become meaningful. Projection mechanisms and identifications have been operating, and the subject is depleted to the extent that something of the subject is found in the object..."[41] When I read Winnicott's writings during my organisational psychology studies, I was struck by the failure of other researchers to pay real attention to his argument: everyone picked up on the importance of transitional objects for children, but hardly anyone paid attention to his acknowledgement that play was just as – if not more – important for the wellbeing of adults.

Another modern psychologist, Christopher Bollas, investigated how humans relate to tangible objects and project ourselves onto these unassuming things. These objects have aesthetic values to us. They could evoke sensory reactions or perhaps even memories and sentiments. He looked at how humans bestow symbolic meanings and emotions upon objects – emotions that we ourselves sometimes do not comprehend[42]. By seeing ourselves within these inanimate objects, we can start to transform ourselves and merge our real selves with our ideal selves.

I had the most riveting conversation with Bollas a few years ago in Singapore. Any consultant, strategist or manager might have winced in disgust had they listened in on our hour-long conversation, for there was no agenda, no logical flow, and nothing in particular to discuss in our meeting – we just talked. That was the beauty of it. The seeming randomness allowed space for creativity and imagination. We talked about objects, how I saw them, how he saw them, how else we could relate to them. We flitted and floated and talked about the red glasses hanging around his neck and what that made me think of. We talked about picture books, bears, my PhD, writing ...We *played*. In this playing, we were thinking. And in this spontaineity we sprouted ideas and new thoughts. I discovered what even *I* didn't know I didn't know. It was the most marvellous conversation and exploration of what objects and play meant to adults because we simply played!

Such is the contribution of these toys to our psychological health, though they are often deemed childish, useless and silly. A certain kind of magic happens when we play. We experience a new kind of freedom. We gain an everyday creativity that beats Picasso's and Shakespeare's, because we find new ways of looking at things and become enlightened as a result.

In this space, I projected the grim issues with which I was dealing onto a third-party object, to make it a safe environment for myself to re-examine my core, without the risk of reigniting my grief and distress. It was so easy because I could experiment. It was so difficult because each realisation brought me closer to my fears.

These objects – whether a bear, a candle, a toy car, a doll – are a remembrance of childhood, and a temporary entrance into our playfulness. Yet, we do not dare walk in. We drool like a kid looking into Santa's workshop, not seeing the door right next to us.

But when we do, we enter a world of delight.

My friend, Ambrose Lee, has run the Toy Museum in Hong Kong for decades[43]. It's stacked with tens of thousands of toys and is tucked away in Prince's Building in the middle of the Central Business District. He now has a warehouse where he stores these toys. He repairs them as well as selling them, from vintage collections to more recent favourites. The emotional attachment to toys is apparent for him, especially when he sees so many fathers coming into the store to buy Star Wars toys with their children. I spoke with him at length for writing an article on play. 'They just want to buy for themselves,' he said. 'It helps them feel like a kid again, to play with toys again.' [44] People from all walks of life drop by during their lunch hours to browse and to relive their childhoods, reinvigorating themselves through playing with GI Joes, Lego, or Care Bears, before heading back to their offices with huge smiles on their faces.

A toy is not just a plaything; it is a good companion for every individual, as toys share all the private moments with the owners. They keep secrets and soak up all the happiness and sadness and loneliness. This is why toys are meaningful only for their owners. Other people sit on the periphery, imagining the sense of warmth and reassurance they get from the toy[45].

Once I realised that I had created a safe space to analyse myself through inanimate objects – and had started to see the world from a different perspective – I began to wonder if toys and objects could hold a similar meaning for others. Most people who heard my idea were derisive and deemed it impossible. The more polite ones would smile and nod. I was determined to prove them wrong.

I soldiered on with the Bearapy concept, developing it into workshops to show people how to play. I helped people increase their self-awareness, de-stress, and find creativity through doing so. All the while this would improve employees' wellbeing. Bearapy started focussing on more than just toy bears. It could be any toy, any animal, any figurine, any object.

When I was first setting out to build Bearapy into a compan that offered educational programmes to raise awareness of mental health, I was dubious. I asked some classmates at my business school to try out the play techniques for me.

We roleplayed with bears. We laughed at our playful voices during the activities. We discussed transitional objects – I found it intriguing that so many did not know what their transitional objects were! Some became so engrossed with Bearapy that I felt they could be ambassadors for my cause, and some found it difficult to play. But whether in denial or not, we all play in some shape or form. Play is proven to be intrinsically linked to relaxation – just take a look at the massive piles of research in psychology, anthropology, sociology and neuroscience that attest to the fact that objects and toys on our desks are much more than props.

And yet we disown our innate abilities to be curious. Toys that once mattered to us end up in storage, recycle bins and garbage dumps.

I have spoken with many individuals about their objects through my work at Bearapy, mostly the objects they keep in the office that aren't actually work-related[46]. Sometimes it would be only a red backpack or a computer case made of a particular fabric. Sometimes it would be animal figurines. The way we unknowingly use toys, particularly in the workplaces, was astounding. I have seen pets, teddies, toy cars, toy figurines, photos, magnets, rocks, toy helicopters and cookie jars crowd out people's work desks. At first glance, most people didn't think twice about these objects; some didn't even remember they had them on their desks! As we chatted, there were proclamations of excitement as people rediscovered their beloved objects, recounting memorable trips or showing off their children's drawings. The aesthetics appealed to their senses. Maybe the objects were pleasant to look at, or perhaps they stirred up happy childhood memories. It was a form of emotional attachment.

There is profound symbolism in these objects. They hold unforgettable moments, wishes and (unfulfilled) dreams within plastic, metal or other materials that, for anyone else, bear no relevance. Some objects have the excuse of being useful and functional, such as a bowl. Others are broken or no longer useful, but still kept.

For example, Frank[47], a 58-year-old male, had a decrepit key from years ago that couldn't be used anymore because the door no longer existed. And yet he kept it on his desk in remembrance of days gone by. In his mind it helped him go through a symbolic door and re-enter a period of time in his memory.

***Figure 15:*** *A key that cannot open any doors (Frank, 58, male).*

I focused on what objects meant in the workplace for executives with toys on their desks. Executives did not think play was appropriate in the workplace, deeming it unprofessional. Not many people liked the word "play" either. Some found the notion strange and had not thought about their desktop displays prior to talking to me. Some chuckled awkwardly when they acknowledged that they had fun when talking to their plants or toy bears. Others were reticent and seemed discomfited to admit that they took the time to clean the thin layer of dust on their figurines. Still others defended their actions by dismissing the objects, or denying that they had any[48].

We experience play through our objects, even if we don't know it or want to admit so. I have talked to many people about their playing with their objects, and many did so while they were thinking or engaged in another activity. Others got up consciously because they needed a break, so they went to water the plant and talk to it, coaxing it to grow and flourish.

It sounds silly or even delusional, yet this is the exact essence of playing, with an element of exaggeration or illusion simply for the momentary enjoyment. People like this interaction. Interactions can be as simple as swivelling a Mont Blanc pen in your hands or rearranging the toys on your desks every two days. People can become absorbed in staring at a small ceramic bowl containing a mélange of keys and coins on their cabinets. In this transient interaction, a thinking space is created, whether for reflection or distraction. It is in this space of play, brought about by the toys and objects around us, that creativity prospers. Winnicott claimed: "perhaps only in playing, the child or adult is free to be creative"[49].

The mere establishment of the Beardom – all my bears with their array of names and personalities – was, in itself, creativity. My creativity was given a voice again.

There is no shame in having toys. There is no shame in needing help. There is no guilt in resting and doing nothing but breathing for the day.

The bears helped me forget about other people's judgment. They helped me do what I enjoyed. Some people thought I was childish to travel with a bear. I dare you to take a photo of a bear sitting on the plane, watching *Dumbo!*

You might think I'm immature, but I don't mind. I see the value in what I am doing – if not for others, at least for my own sanity and soul. I have confidence in this. There is a child in me, an inner child that could be so powerful if only I would let her express herself.

We envy the freedom that children have to just play, to just be. But most adults cannot not be occupied with toys, even if there is a secret wish to

**Figure 16:** *Muddie watching Dumbo.*

do so. There are more important milestones to achieve – and targets to beat.

In the end, the individual is the one responsible for imprisoning their inner child.

And this is the essence of Bearapy – to free that inner child from the constraints we place on ourselves. It is to find our playfulness once again, whatever it may mean for us. In doing so, we are doing ourselves a favour – both by unleashing the creativity inside of us and in the prevention of burnout, because we find situations less stressful. In doing so, we can save ourselves from the brink of despair, depression, and perhaps even suicide.

We might have stopped collecting matchboxes as adults, but we now collect boxes painted with famous artwork. We collect souvenirs from each museum we visit, as a mature cover up for our playfulness. We buy fridge magnets, postcards, reindeer toys; we play with the keyrings on our desks because they help us to think.

'Declutter,' we say, suppressing the very essence of how objects silently support us in our endeavours. Some we throw away and some we keep, even though they are now dilapidated, hoping that maybe our kids might value our toy collections one day.

**Figure 17:** *Chillie.*
*Chillie takes it easy and has lots of time to simply sit and do nothing. He never plans for anything and adopts a "bears will figure it out" attitude with every obstacle that comes his way. His life goal is to get Beezie, Scruffie, and Fuzzie to stop, breathe, and see the humorous side of life.*

# CHAPTER 10

# PLAY

I jumped from one sofa to the next. I did a forward roll on the floor and flew up onto the sofa again. I was Donatello, the purple Teenage Mutant Ninja Turtle, ready to dole out justice in my imaginary world. We had emigrated to Australia from Hong Kong when I was young. I was seven years old and had lots of free time at home, because school in Perth did not entail homework. So I played.

I didn't know that I needed to make the most of this time. It came to an end upon our return to China a few years later.

What is play? It is anything and everything you want it to be. Any time. Anywhere.

In a sense, it's not tangible. It could be daydreaming, reading a book, dancing in the shower, singing to oneself on the bus, doodling, watching a beetle crawl from one blade of grass to the next ...

*Homo Ludens* (the human being who plays) by Johan Huizinga is one of my favourite books about play . It details the following elements of play, which are often referenced in research. So, what makes "play", according to Huizinga?

1. It is fully absorbing

2. It is intrinsically motivated

3. It includes elements of uncertainty or surprise

4. It involves a sense of illusion or exaggeration

In *The Ambiguity of Play*[51], the late Brian Sutton-Smith comments that play is ambiguous because it is so personal. In an email thread in which I was interviewing him for an article on play, Vice President for Studies at the Strong National Museum of Play in New York, Scott Eberle, states that play is fun[52]. Eberle was instrumental in setting up the Museum of Play, which contains artefacts designed to inspire adults to play. Other academics discussed playfulness as a personality disposition[53], encompassing the traits of spontaneity, expressiveness, fun, creativity, and silliness[54]. The definitions are endless.

For the same article on playfulness, I had the opportunity to speak with Professor Stuart Brown (President and Founder of the National Institute of Play) and get his advice and viewpoints on why play was so vital to our health. Brown explained that play has no purpose in itself other than for the sake of playing. However, this doesn't mean that there aren't any positive outcomes[55]. Take for instance, singing and dancing. If we sing and dance because we simply enjoy it, then that is play, and the positive by-product could be burning some calories. However, if we sing and dance in order to get applause or attention, then it may become a show or entertainment. In this case, spontaneous "playfulness" is no longer playful, because then we are focused on reaching a specific purpose or goal.

But whatever the dichotomies, the definitions, or the juxtapositions, they are not my main concern. Neither is whether play is relative to work or one and the same. I am appalled at how many of us have forgotten to play. At first, I thought that it was only those who grew up in competitive Hong Kong, but then my experience extended to those growing up in mainland China, Singapore, the US, and then the rest of the world. And of course, there are also those who are playful in all these countries.

Play comes in many forms. Perhaps the most typical would be:

1. Solitary play: playing alone

2. Social play: playing with others

3. Object play: manipulating some type of object, could
   be done with others or on one's own

I am most interested in object play because it was a stuffed toy bear that helped me to rediscover myself through play. Yet, as I've said before, Bearapy today is not fixated only on bears. It works with whatever toy or object might work for the cause of preventing stress and burnout. When I mention play and the ideas of Bearapy – whether it be in a corporate environment, a professional network, at a social dinner, a talk, or a business school – the immediate response is generally one of the following:

1. Is this for children? You should do it with kids.

2. Is this for creative industries?

3. I come to work, not to play!

These were comments from all sorts of people from all walks of life; people whom I would have assumed to be open-minded, educated, and willing to try new things. My unconscious bias, indeed! The only sympathisers were teachers and occasionally a few people in the audience who had experienced the same depressive journey or suppression of creativity. Bernard de Koven, author of *The Playful Path*[56], said profoundly in his TEDx talk[57] that "we do not lose our playfulness, we just do not access it." Many of us forget to play or have forgotten *how* to play: there were times when rolling in the mud would send us into hysterics. So why don't we do that anymore?

In the workplace we dismiss play as childish because it scares us. We are afraid that it makes us vulnerable, because being playful exposes the parts of us hidden under the power suits, the meeting agendas, and the titles of authority. Even picking up this book out of interest, and then putting it down again because it seems unproductive, is a dismissal.

The idea of playing in the office was not entirely novel, but it did seem strange to the executives and leaders I talked to, as if it made sense in academic journals but not so much in real life. They did not work for Google, and so some claimed that such vibrant offices were "over the top". Perhaps it's because, as adults, we believe that we must "grow up" and "graduate" from playing.

What about camouflage? There are those who buy bears that have T-shirts on them which feature a company logo. Perhaps this represents the owner's suppressed desire for what was once a much-loved activity in childhood – but also their fear that society would not approve – and so they disguise play as a corporate gift.

Why is play seen as unprofessional? I tried to find out when researching for my executive master's thesis in 2015 when I was completing my organisational psychology degree[58] and during Bearapy workshops that I created and presented over the last few years. People could not agree on an answer, or even begin to understand their own stereotypes. Sofia, for example, is the Finance Controller of an oil company based in Central Asia. She was one of those people who were wary that toys made her look "childish" and "unprofessional," and would not match the identity she presented to society. She has a toy bear to whom she defers when she's had a hard day. She murmurs to the bear, 'I have had enough. You are in charge now!' Although the bear is her protector, she keeps it at a distance on a cabinet next to

**Figure 18:** *Sofia (34, female) puts her bears in charge of the office sometimes.*

117

her desk. She told me she did not want anyone from outside to see her as "some secretary." She was a senior executive and she thought it was not appropriate to have all this stuff.[59]

I empathised with Sofia. We had both imposed on ourselves what we thought society deemed as acceptable and appropriate for our roles. We had adopted and internalised our unspoken ways without questioning them – or rather, left the questioning for when no one was listening. So we hid our playing, alluding to it only in ways that would not shatter our mature, professional façades. Sofia shared, 'Because I thought that nobody should see this in the office, I put him on the chair, hidden away. And then I say to him, "You take care of this place."'

It's not just women, though. Noah is a 40-year-old consultant[60]. He had a stress ball with a red heart on it that travelled with him. He brought it with him each time he moved offices. 'I think a red heart is too much in a professional setting. I don't find it professional enough. So I keep this red heart hidden away.' However, when I probed him on why it was "not professional enough", Noah was uncertain.

When asked to think about why we think the way we do, we are astounded by how blind we have been when following the herd, conforming, and acquiescing. Sofia and Noah discounted the significance of the toys on their desks, or even denied that they had any. They referred to them as "silly" or "really stupid." Sofia would even pretend the bear wasn't hers, justifying the presence of the bear as a gift from the company in order to keep her image intact.

The façades we adopt in order to be seen in a certain light – intellectual, powerful, knowledgeable, efficient, and effective – are there in order to make us feel safe. Being playful could make us look silly. It could cause us to let down our guards. It would force us to be ourselves in that split second, and therefore expose us to the judgement and rejection of others. We don these masks for a reason: if we continue in our masquerade, any judgment or rejection is pointed towards the painted faces we wear, and not our true selves. Thus, we feel safe. We don't have to take it personally. We could change, chameleon-like, to be "different". We could "change", "improve." I once found these words to be good reason to give up playing.

This is maybe one reason why companies' employee assistance programmes are not always effective. We have a pretence we think need to keep up, a smokescreen of professionalism. *I can't let them find me out,* we think. But the chances are that "they" are equally concerned that we will find *them* out. The main reason, in my not-so-humble opinion, is that we are too scared to face ourselves. It's not the companies' faults; if anything they are our allies, because they want us to be healthy and productive.

And so we rely on permission from others to be playful, most typically in team-building exercises, in amusement parks, or on holiday, since in those situations everyone else is doing the same thing. There may even be a facilitator in each of these circumstances, there to engage and direct us to play. This pacifies us – if it all becomes silly, it's not our fault, but that of the facilitator.

This brings me to the interesting topic of games. When I mention "playfulness," I get a lot of people asking me to show them a game. A game in itself is not playfulness, though taking part in one could in fact be the easiest form of play.

I can see how games can be synonymous with play, but they do limit our understanding of what it is. With a game, there are rules, parameters, steps, an end goal. The game itself gives us the permission we need to play. And so we rely on the game, perhaps becoming over-dependent on it, and forget that we can be playful without that framework.

When we were kids, we had no qualms about what others thought. Whatever we drew, we were proud of. It was just what it was: a drawing. My daughter is four years old. Since she was a toddler, she would scribble and squiggle on paper endlessly, or splash paint on canvas paper. They bore no form in my eyes, and I would not know what she was drawing. Yet, in her mind she was drawing gardens and flowers and carrots and squirrels. She drew a rocket landing in the midst of it all. She did not care whether I saw the same thing or not. She found intrinsic pleasure and enjoyment, and did not care less what I thought, nor did she start critiquing the brushstrokes or use of colour. Many adults prohibit ourselves from this same freedom. We reject the idea that we should be different, and instead embrace the "normal". We hide in week-long retreats in different exotic places on Earth in order to sing, dance, and draw again. We are looking for our long-neglected playful selves, while masking our playfulness under the guise of "art therapy" or "detoxing".

Why do we need permission to play? It's a faulty premise. What we think is normal is not!

I tried to coax business executives to let their employees play. Typically, they were needlessly concerned that play could distract from work[61], and that it was unprofessional[62] and immature[63]. This was because they did not understand play. My own neglect of playfulness prior to my depression meant that I ignored the inherent capabilities I was born with. Children know how to play, for it is an innate ability, and the only ones interfering are adults.

Play is a developmental skill for learning[64] and contributes to leadership development[65]. Play positively impacts health and wellbeing by relieving stress, building social bonds and inspiring creativity[66]. A healthy workspace is dependent on play and fun[67]. Events like company dinners, employee appreciation weeks, and charity events are known to boost staff morale, promote group collaboration, and encourage loyalty towards the organisation[68]. Fun can enhance employees' creativity, enabling them to devise brighter and better solutions[69].

Play extends beyond psychology and psychotherapy. Donald Winnicott's hope was to spread the good news instead of confining play to psychoanalysis, stating that "*it is play that is the universal*, and that belongs to health: playing facilitates growth and therefore health; playing leads into group relationships ..."[70]

Through playing, we test possibilities. Play opens our minds to "fantasies, ideas, and the world's possibilities in a way that continually allows for the surprising, the original, and the new"[71], creating space for expression[72].

When I speak about playfulness, I mean it in an inner sense. A common query I get in workshops is about the difference between mindfulness and playfulness.

Modern-day mindfulness seems be undertaken as a means to its own end. I once overheard a person saying to someone else, 'How mindful are you? You are not mindful enough,' as if there was a way to quantify the inner state of mind. Mindfulness has become its own standard and benchmark.

The way I understand mindfulness is to see it as way to ponder the world around us. It helps us to detach ourselves from attachments and be more in touch with ourselves and the sentiments of others. It gives a voice to our intuitions and allows us to recognise how we feel at the present moment.

So, mindfulness is to be aware. Playfulness is thinking. It is a language in itself, something that everyone has inside of them. It is innate. An expression. A communication. An imagination. A knowing. This was how we learn as kids, and how we continue to learn as adults. This is why I skip down the road, why I sit and stare out the window. This is why I founded Bearapy and expanded it beyond my own bears. I wanted to help organisations, teams, and individuals find their playfulness, so that mental health becomes engraved into company culture and is no longer just a KPI that the Human Resources department has to fulfil.

Through play, groups bond and connect, building team cohesion. Organisations with a playful culture are more productive and have a more engaged and healthy employee population. Playfulness is a basic tenet and fabric of society.

There are so many academic references on playfulness. Most academic scholars do not agree on the exact definitions or assessment of play, though they probably do not agree on much anyways. They do, however, concur that play is essential for a healthy life. So, when someone gets up from the desk to fly a remote-controlled helicopter around the office, pushes toy cars back and forth on the desktop or moves a bear's arms and legs around, just accept that he or she is playing because these are acts that are fully absorbing, self-motivated, surprising, and include a sense of illusion. For some, playfulness might mean just a mere glance at a postcard, a simple flick of a pen, or patting a flamingo figurine built with mini blocks, while thinking about next year's strategy. If these acts are enjoyable, absorbing, and self-motivated, then this must be play.

There is nothing truly stopping us from having serious fun in order to take a break from our busy lives. There is nothing stopping us from entertaining ourselves with witty humour during boring train rides.

There is so much research on playfulness. But how are we *using* the research? Is it only in play museums or designated places? Can we not find a way to use what we have in the real world? Can we give ourselves permission to just be *us*?

*We* are the only ones who are stopping ourselves from doing this. Our critical selves. Our insecure selves.

Boring, dull, rigid, anal, and stuck up men and women like me need to learn how to play again. We need to get over ourselves and be daring and open-minded enough to try something we have spent so long resisting. Let's bring playfulness back to the forefront of our conscious minds. We should engage in play consciously, and then it becomes a habit again.

Playing with toys and objects is who I really am. Displaying my vulnerability and exposing this part of myself without fear of others' judgment was the first step to self-healing. It is not an upward trajectory. Vulnerability is a bumpy ride. It can lead us to self-hatred, but discovering its power can also be euphoric.

Showing vulnerability does not just mean exposing weaknesses. It's not just saying, 'I admit this is how I am weak.' It's a trap that the Chinese translation of "vulnerable" is the same as the one for "weakness" – and thus the Chinese population seem unable to come to terms with accepting vulnerability. Perhaps this is also why playing seems like a juxtaposition to being strong, because playing exposes our vulnerability.

But the way I understand it, it helps us to show our competencies, inner beauty, worries, and dreams.

I had no illusion that my bears were alive. But they *were* alive in my depressed mind, where my imagination knew no boundaries. My mental wellbeing hinged on this interface between reality and illusion, created through play. I know that in my rational mind, the bears were merely objects. But I allowed my rational mind to break free from the chains I had put on them, and so the rationality in me ran free – creating, crafting, trying, learning, experimenting. I became alive again.

In the agony, I saw rainbow sparkles. And I drifted out of depression with new ideas of what I could do now that my banker life had disintegrated. This is why I talked to my bears. I played with them, hung out with them, nuzzled up to them. This was the enthusiasm I once had as a child. In regressing, I progressed.

*Play is more than mindfulness. Put simply, it is an awareness – an awareness of ourselves, our thoughts and our emotions. Through play, we can contemplate our relationships with the environment and the world.*

*Playfulness is to breathe, to allow our minds to wander aimlessly, to make sense of our experiences.*

*Playfulness is an enlightenment – not just about what games to play, but how to be playful in our individual ways.*

*Playfulness is a means – we find the power of play in our individual lives. We use it for learning, creativity, self-awareness, and wellbeing.*

*Playfulness is an attitude. When we become playful beings, we view the world and all its intricacies with a different lens, freeing ourselves from ourselves.*

*Playfulness is a diamond, cut into a million facets. Each of its sides reflect, refract, and shine in splendour.*

*Playful helps you accept yourself. It helps you say 'I am enough.'*

**Figure 19:** *Snuggie.*
*Snuggie's mission in life is to find those who are sad and lonely and give them a snuggle or three.*

# CHAPTER 11

# PLAY AND EMOTIONS

Floppie and the bears taught me how to feel. The moment I accepted I was depressed, I could address the feelings of depression. This gave me some energy to dissect what was beneath it all. I wrote about this on my blog, and writing was part of the therapy prescribed.

The bears helped put words to my feelings and to express them. They helped me articulate my inner thoughts. First off though, I had to know what I was feeling. Through my depression and my Bearapy work thereafter, I realised that so many of us don't know how we feel either. It is as if we have closed down the ability to feel. To be able to feel is paramount, because these emotions send us a message about ourselves. And if we are able to articulate how we feel, then perhaps we are one step closer to saying, 'I do not feel well; I need help,' especially when we are nearing burnout and depression. It might just be able to keep us from the edge. Part of it is admitting, 'I'm not okay.'

To help myself and others find playful ways of expressing our feelings, I launched a Bearapy online campaign for World Health Day 2017. Inspired by my story, my friend Dai Cameron[73] drew bear pictures for me to use freely for the Bearapy mission.

I posted one a day on social media platforms for a few days, asking people to leave comments about what they thought the bear was feeling.

I had various comments, such as:

"Lost."

"Longing."

"Regret."

"Sad."

"Excitement for the future."

*Figure 20: Bear on boat.*

My favourite one came from Instagram: the bear had lost his fishing rod after a fight with a whale shark, and so he had to go home and buy a new one, wasting a whole day. What humorous creativity! Quite a few people wrote to me and asked, 'Is that a tear on his face?' A few others told me that was his cheek or his smile.

As for me, I think the bear on the boat feels both excited and lonely at the same time.

Some thought that this bear on the beach was feeling exhilarated and having fun. A few remarked that the bear looked alone because he was playing on his own. Amusingly, one of my friends commented that the bear was enjoying himself so much that he didn't notice he was naked! What a carefree spirit the bear has!

*Figure 21: Bear on the beach.*

Why were there such different responses from the same picture? Well, it is simply because we look at it from our unique perspectives, history, and biases.

What we see in these pictures is just the first step. The bigger question is *why* do we see the bear like that? *Why* do we think the bear feels longing and excitement and not regret? What does it reflect from inside us?

We project our own feelings onto others and onto objects around us. We imagine them to feel as we feel. Part of this might be to protect ourselves from some emotions that are not so pleasant. We carry our own assumptions with us, based on our past experiences. Our emotional states, learnt perceptions of the world, and conscious and subconscious thoughts lead us to see the same picture differently from others.

Identifying emotions is the critical first step. To express them, even to ourselves, is the next challenge. It is not an easy process. But, when we are playful, the process becomes easier. This playfulness can take on many forms.

In a Bearapy workshop with teenagers at an international school for World Mental Health Day 2017, we discussed emotional awareness and mental health. It seemed a bit dry to simply talk about emotions, so I encouraged them all to play. I asked them to draw pictures to represent different emotions. What would it feel like to feel angry, alone, disappointed, happy, peaceful? What are the other words for emotions? As they drew, they also had fun. They freed up their thoughts and freely associated with their emotions.

Playing fosters emotional awareness. It helps us access our emotional vulnerabilities. And reminds us that we can express these emotions. It might be taxing for some to say in a straightforward manner, 'I am stressed.' Adding a bit of play makes such expression less threatening.

Take the song 'If you're happy and you know it,' for instance. Many people would know the song and be able to hum it. Parents know it off by heart. *If you're happy and you know it, clap your hands … stamp your feet … turn around … say hurray …*

However, we are not happy all the time. Sometimes we are sad, furious, disappointed, lonely, nostalgic, insecure ... But there are no songs about it. It's a subtle hint to us that only when we are happy should we express it for the world to see. Otherwise, we're to keep it under wraps. So, I decided to change the lyrics for a TEDx talk[74] on playfulness and emotional awareness:

*If you're happy and you know it, clap your hands ...*

*If you're angry and you know it, stamp your feet ...*

*If you're stressed and you know it, say "Aiiiii!" ...*

Same song, different lyrics. There were similar or different physical behaviours to express the emotions. Suddenly it became fun, and we laughed even though we were singing about how stressed we were.

We hide our real emotions – the disappointments, the frustrations, the sorrow – for fear of judgment and backlash of non-conformity. Before my depression, I denied my emotions. Worse than this, I had no idea how I was feeling beyond "fine" and "okay," and that's not a good emotional vocabulary at all. When I cried, I cried behind closed doors.

These few minutes of play allowed us to see that it was okay to be not okay, that there are creative, playful, fun ways of expressing ourselves. There's a whole spectrum and intensity of emotions. We can sing to ourselves, to our toys, with our friends. Being playful means that we can test assumptions, push ourselves out of the comfort zone. And when we project our feelings on to a third party like a bear or bear picture, it starts to become easier to accept: it is okay to not be okay.

For those who would like to dig deeper, below are some pictures of unassuming bears. They can be windows into our unconscious worries, anxieties, and fears.

*Figure 22: Orange bear.*

Is this bear falling down, or taking his first step towards something new?

*Figure 23: Bear and ball.*

Is this bear, balancing the ball, feeling relaxed? Or is he juggling too much, with lots of things on his plate?

*Figure 24: Red bear.*

Is this red bear wishing he could go to bed instead of working on his computer? Or is he enjoying composing electronic music? Or, is he feeling nostalgic looking through old photos?

How is this yellow bear feeling? Is he feeling trepidation, worry, serenity? Is he feeling mischievous?

*Figure 25: Yellow bear.*

What other stories can you come up with? Let your imagination run wild.

Whatever your answer, ask yourself: why do you see the bear as such?

When asked this question, some might flee the scene. Some might say it's because that's how the bear was drawn. Perhaps ... and there is in part, our own perspectives, emotions, thoughts, biases, and history in the answer. Many of us may feel judged, rejected, or inadequate about our own answers, but perhaps the first step is to answer to ourselves. Let the unconscious thoughts that are submerged under the water float up, so that we can see ourselves. Our full selves.

We can take responsibility for our thoughts and feelings, which then make them less complicated to identify, acknowledge, confront, and express.

Being able to express the range of emotions through play makes it less threatening to accept help. We are then able to ask for it when we are met with our down days, before we hit melancholy and despair. Talking about your emotions – and having the courage to face up to them – is the first step towards seeking help, especially for issues like depression. Mental health issues and burnout can be Prevented, if we can be honest with ourselves.

*Figure 26:* Fumblie.

*Fumblie thinks he's a rhino and charges at people. He is very innocent and is happy to simply be himself.*

# CHAPTER 12

# PLAY AND FEARS

Children are adept at expressing their feelings with no reservations. They swing like a pendulum between rage and ecstasy in split seconds. Adults lose their directness because of fear. There is no shortage of literature about fear and how to overcome it, but I am not sure there is a panacea to fear. In fact, fear protects us sometimes. Fear triggers alarm bells, activating our survival instincts to preserve ourselves. We then decide to run from the situation, fight it, or simply freeze – for example, if a grizzly bear is about to attack us in the deep forest.

This topic of fear is fascinating. We all have it. We try to get rid of it, desensitise ourselves, ignore it, hide it under the carpet.

I want to face my fears – and use them.

Sigmund Freud, considered the forefather of psychoanalysis, uses a metaphor about conscious thoughts and behaviours. He describes them as the tip of the iceberg[75]. Below our consciousness, underneath the surface of the water, sit our subconscious thoughts and emotions, such as memories. These are easily retrievable. Research shows that the subconscious processes about 200 times more data than our consciousness. It is a powerful driver.

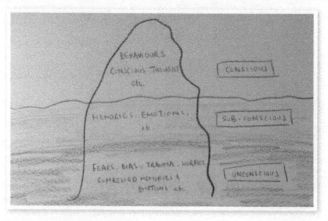

**Figure 27:** *Freud's iceberg.*

Whereas subconscious memories regularly come into our conscious awareness, the *unconscious* feelings and assumptions are hidden beneath the subconscious layer – this is where fears, biases, worries, traumas, and suppressed emotions reside without our awareness. And yet they are the key motors that drive our overt behaviours. These are harder to access.

The unconscious is where the root of my fear lies. Here are the ideas that I have internalised over the last 37 years on Earth. These ideas might be based on seemingly innocent events that happened in my childhood, or offhand remarks made to me during my adulthood. Whatever the events, they've been stored into long-term memory and eventually filed into my unconsciousness as traumatic experiences. This results in fear. It is a mystery to me, because I don't know how it works exactly. I just know it does.

I've done lots of introspection over the years – throughout my depression, during my recovery, back in the slumps, and on the up again. As Bearapy evolved over the last two years into a business proposition, I reflected again on my fears, because I was so scared of failing and being inadequate – again.

I drew a picture of my fears[76]. At the top of the iceberg were my overt behaviours – including acting professional, disengaged, strong and cached behind my mask. Subconsciously I believed that I needed to do things myself to show how strong I was. But I believed I was not good enough. I had long wanted to change the habit of filling up my schedule, to take time to just be with myself and manage my mental energy. I knew that if I took more time to take care of myself, my whole being would flourish. Yet, time and time again, I filled my schedules with appointments, things to do, people to see. I assumed that I was stupid and that people wouldn't like me if I said no to appointments and plans. But why did I do the opposite of what is good for me? Why would I take care of others first, to my own detriment?

**Figure 28:** *Nochie's fears.*

All of these beliefs and assumptions were driven by fears that were so steeped into my unconsciousness that they rooted the iceberg onto the seabed. If I dug beneath it, I would reach the core of lava at the centre of the earth.

Carl Jung described the unconscious aspect of our personalities – the ones that our conscious egos do not want to admit[77] – as a shadow. I was fearful of dependence, intimacy, or abandonment. Most of all, I was afraid to be worthless. It would make living meaningless.

*Figure 29: Little Nochie.*

Then what would make life worth living? How would I decide for myself? How could I shake myself off from the shadows of the past, most of which I had created for myself?

We read a lot about childhood development, the different stages, and the corresponding skills a child acquires from birth. Surprisingly or not, adults have stages of development too. Robert Kegan[78] and Daniel Levinson[79] have influenced this area of study, and what resonates with me is that as we progress through adulthood, we come to realise that many of our behaviours used to be geared towards meeting others' expectations. Once we are able to let go of those expectations, we start to live for ourselves.

This concept of being the author of your own life has been moulded by many psychologists over the years. There's so much theory that I sometimes cannot digest it. But this is what I understand to be behind the concept: at this stage of maturity in my adult development, I can start to be myself. I am my inner child. Little Nochie can come out to play and not mind what others think. She can stay in her Bear Cave if she is tired. She feels no pressure to prove her adequacy, and she isn't worried that others will leave her if she doesn't go along and play however others want her to. She is not a court jester dancing a show for others to see. She is not there for others to judge. There is no need for masks.

This is where my fears can be transformed: I can now engage with my heart and be emotionally available. This is the answer to my fears. I may always have them, but I now have the choice to act on them or not. I can catch myself making automatic responses due to fear. I can use the fear.

***Figure 30:*** *Little Nochie 2.*

Playfulness also contributed to me working through my fears. Through playing again, I started to realise that I was scared to play, because I was concerned with how silly I might look to others, whether they would still respect me, and how they would judge me. I saw how playing manifested my conscious and unconscious thoughts and feelings, and how the processes of playing were both conscious and unconscious. I used Freud's analogy of the iceberg as base to come up with my own Playfulness Iceberg.

135

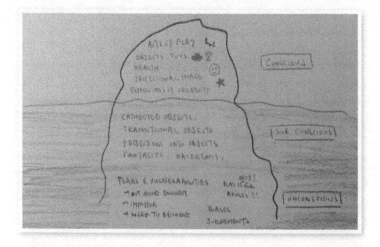

**Figure 31:** *Playfulness Iceberg.*

The tip of the iceberg above water is what we can see (like the conscious mind). This could include climbing up slides, throwing a ball, playing games like hide-and-seek. This is the product of your creativity and innovation. The tip of the iceberg also includes your appearance and the aspects of it that indicate your level of health, like your complexion, posture, fitness or lack thereof. It could also include the image that you put out to others.

The layer immediately below the surface of the Playfulness Iceberg (the subconscious layer) houses your cathected objects and transitional objects, objects onto which we project our feelings and into which we invest emotion. These objects mean something to us emotionally and serve as mementos or inspiration. These objects might not stay at the forefront of our minds, and can even be neglected on a daily basis. These objects give us life, vitality, and imagination. Silently, loyally, they keep us from feeling overwhelmed and burnt out – if only we would listen to them.

Deep down on the Playfulness Iceberg is your unconscious, where your fears lie – fears of rejection, inadequacy, loneliness, and irrelevance. This is also where your resistance to play may be. This is why you assume that as adults we shouldn't play anymore or that play is a waste of time. This is why you think others would ridicule you if you were playful. But here is also where playful childhood memories are stored. Mostly they're repressed because you think they don't matter anymore. However, through the process of playing – especially with the inspiration of objects and toys – you unearth these memories and valuable insights. You see the world through the enthusiastic eyes of a child. This is why playing is vital to your health.

Playing games, playing with toys, and swinging on trees are all behaviours that look innocent. But they are much more instrumental to us than we think. In the act of play, we discover how we really feel. We remember how we used to feel and we come alive. In the playful mind, we are opened to new ideas. We are curious, energetic, and able to confront our fears and concerns. After playing, we feel refreshed and rejuvenated, ready for the next challenge.

Playing gives us a valuable insight into our emotions: why do we feel a certain way? What are the thoughts behind these emotions? What are our worries and uncertainties?

We look to others to give us the answer, forgetting – and unable to accept – that we ourselves hold the insights.

**Figure 32:** *Scruffie.*
*Scruffie is anal about every little perfection in life, and obsessive about the way his long fur is groomed. He picks on the defects of the other bears and is overly critical and judgmental. As a result, he doesn't yet have many bear friends.*

137

# CHAPTER 13

# PLAY AND INTROSPECTION

I am judgmental.

When I was 15 years old, I attended a girls' high school in Hong Kong. I went to school as normal, but on one particular day there was a disconcerting dreariness in the air. A few teachers looked like they had been crying all weekend. Finally, someone was brave enough to break the silence – a popular girl who was senior to me, had perfect grades, and excelled in other subjects such as drama and debate, had taken her own life. I had been on the debate team with her and I loved her big smiles and amicable disposition.

I could still remember that moment, sitting on the hard bench in the school chapel for her memorial service, thinking, *I will never kill myself*. I thought she was foolish to have given up her life.

Fifteen years later, I nearly did. In fact, I tried a few times, and each time I was disappointed and frustrated at myself for not even being able to complete this task. I questioned my competence.

Now that I can empathise, I realise how judgmental I used to be towards those who took their own lives. My heart was closed to their stories. I judged, as others judged me.

The judgment that killing ourselves is wrong seems to be one reason why we cannot admit our suicidal thoughts to others. Judgment is all around us, and we strive to keep up the image, especially the "perfect" one on social media.

"So honoured to eat this gluten-free, organic, home-baked, amazing pie," we type. "Life is great!"

Is it? Behind screens, we often suffer inside.

Suppression and denial were two of the triggers for my depression. I was too proud to look for, or accept, help. But depression cleared the mist before my eyes and defogged my heart so I could feel again. I slobbed, threw tantrums, and raged. I got in touch with injustice, vindication, love, pity, alienation, kindness, guilt, aggression, and gentleness. It was then that I understood that unless you can identify your emotions, you tread towards depression. If you are already struggling with depression, not acknowledging how you feel stops you from asking for help, and this reinforces the vicious cycle.

To learn to confront one's emotions – especially those that we are unwilling to face – is not easy. Such is the barrier in asking for help when in a depressed state of mind. We are wrought with guilt, shame, embarrassment, and humiliation. There is immense fear in asking for help, for fear of being rejected – or worse, ridiculed. Many suffer in silence as a result.

Playing taught me to empathise again, because I saw what it was like for me to access the unpleasant parts of myself. Playing taught me to introspect, to ponder, and to reflect upon my actions and unconscious drivers.

The art of introspection is difficult. It requires immense energy; it requires us to go through unpleasant emotions. And it is unnerving when we realise that there are no "right" or "wrong" answers, and that it is up to us, ourselves, to decide. That is the frightening bit.

It was like the bear pictures in the previous chapters. Some people asked me what the "right" answers were with regards to these pictures. There were none. There were no wrong answers either. Once upon a time I wanted clear-cut answers too. I wanted a well-defined explanation of right and wrong. Smoking was wrong, drugs were wrong, sex before marriage was wrong, and suicide was wrong. But now I know that how I feel is how I feel. It is subjective, individual, independent. Our thoughts and emotions are all our own.

I thought about this girl from high school many times during my depression. Another friend from Japan, who encouraged me throughout my plight, decided to take her own life at the time I was emerging from my depression. I don't know whether she had depression, and I don't know what propelled her to take her life. People commented on how much of a loss it was, how sad, how she shouldn't have done it, how she could have sought help. When thinking rationally, that all makes sense. But when you feel like you're buried under 50 feet of snow, feeling cold, helpless and blinded by depression, none of this is so apparent. Hopelessness overtook me when I was depressed. I was unable to control the tsunami of desolation. The only way out was death.

*No one would ever know we had depression, until they came to our funerals.*

This is why we need to talk and listen, without telling someone 'You shouldn't decide to kill yourself because it will make me sad.' Your sadness is not my cross to carry. Let us all take responsibility for our own feelings. Let us find

**Figure 33:** *Grizzly Bear.*

our own playful spaces to express ourselves with safety, even if we only express our feelings to ourselves.

We need to be honest with ourselves. We need to find out what we do not know we do not know.

We need to face our inner bears. Who are we inside? What are the aspects of ourselves that we don't want to face? This is all achieved through play. We can include a bit of fantasy and a bit of reality. We can use transitional objects to help ourselves get into a playful space. It is a channel, a medium.

The key is being able to search within ourselves. The crux is to find our inner playfulness again. It is possible to de-stress as a white-collar worker or an entrepreneur. Learning to play again saved my adult life. We talk about play as if it is something only children can do.

Play it is so simple, so complex, so pure. Let's break the taboo surrounding it, for our own sanity's sake.

Grant yourself the permission to play. Help each other to play and people will join in.

Play is not an escape. Rather, it asks us to reflect and engage with ourselves on a deeper level. Those who do it naturally do not think about it, and those who do not do it naturally discard it.

**Figure 34:** *Crummie.*
*Crummie can often be heard saying 'I'm so annoyed!' He is cynical and critical. He is annoyed easily, especially at what he considers stupidity. He has super high standards and expectations. He thinks he can do better than the other bears and goes around poking fingers at them, all the while forgetting to look inwards at himself.*

# THE ADULT-CHILD

"The reasonable man (woman) adapts himself (herself) to the world: the unreasonable one persists in trying to adapt the world to himself (herself). Therefore, all progress depends on the unreasonable man (woman)."

George Bernard Shaw[80]

CHAPTER 14

# FISH FACE

Timmie got a promotion at his work around 2011. I said congratulations, but the bears had different thoughts:

Proudie: *I am proud of you!*

Floozie: *Who are you again?*

Floppie: *Zzzzzzz (fast asleep – again).*

Slurpie: *I would love to go to work with you! (Big lopsided grin).*

Crummie: *What took you so long? (Annoyed).*

Gurie: *Inner peace is independent of status and titles.*

Punkie: *It wasn't me who stole all your new business cards!*

This was the same event, but there were different responses. I wrote them down for Timmie and stuck it on to his computer. It took me 30 seconds. It was funny and fun for me. I giggled, and then went about my day. He read the note in under a minute, laughed, and also continued on his day. Playing took less than a minute.

A playful mindset can go a long way to prevent burnout at work. It is possible to be playful at work – play and work do not cancel each other out! Rather, play and work reinforce each other. They can be one and the same. Playful executives become more productive in the workplace!

So many people have asked me how to become playful. I find this a strange question, because I believe everyone is playful. They've just forgotten how, perhaps. When was the last time you played London Bridge is Falling Down or Musical Chairs? Seriously! These games are seen to be for five-year-olds, but I'm 30!

Those who play do it naturally and do not think about it. Those who don't play naturally despise it, discarding it as useless and a waste of time.

Fortunately, not all adults think so. Bill was a senior executive responsible for recruitment and talent management of an international hotel group. He saw the relevance of playfulness with stress management. His team in China was stressed, snowed under. He asked me to help. My mandate was to help them relax. They had been through a series of stress management workshops, time management workshops, and every kind of training possible. So how could I give them more skills than they already possessed, and not stress them out by having to learn yet another thing? I decided to play with them.[81]

For two half-days, we played. There were no PowerPoint presentations, no notes, no lectures. I gave them a small piece of homework prior to meeting them; I asked them to think about what they played with when they were kids. Given that they were of a particular generation, the majority of the responses were "throwing sandbags at each other." With the convenience of Taobao, the giant e-commerce store in China, I found small sandbags at a low cost, took them to the hotel conference room, and gave them to the group of executives. There was an awkward moment as they looked at each other, unsure of what to do. They stood gingerly. Then one woman picked up a sandbag and said, 'Watch, this is how we do it!' and threw it at a colleague. There were a few snickers and still some nervousness. Then one of them decided to make the Head of the Region stand in the middle while everyone else threw sandbags at him. The room broke into hysterical laughter as they played a game they all knew, dodging the sandbags, chucking them at one another in camaraderie. It was an amicable way to lash out their stress at their boss.

'But surely we cannot play this in the office?' they asked.

'Why not?' I asked them.

'Well, it would be inappropriate,' they responded.

'Who said so?' I pressed on.

They looked at each other, unable to answer the question. I surmised that deep inside, they knew that it was they themselves who thought it was inappropriate. But instead of being self-determined, they relied on an external source – me, in this case – to give them permission to play. I had to give them permission to do something that was completely their own.

We often look to others, usually those in authority, to give us permission to do things. That way, if anything goes wrong, we can blame other people. 'Well, it wasn't my idea to throw sandbags at my colleague in the next cubicle.'

On the next half a day, I asked them to bring something from their work desks that was not work related. One brought a dragon toy, another brought a teddy bear, and one a business card case, a souvenir from a trip. I asked them to think about an issue they were facing at work. Then I asked them to talk to the toy they brought. The toy's only response would be to ask "why" to everything they said. They looked at me like it was the most outrageous request they had ever heard, like I was too bizarre.

Perhaps I was. In some ways, I had not entirely planned for the few hours. I was choosing to let my playful self take precedence, to see what might come out of it. They humoured me, opened their minds and tried to do what I requested of them. They tried to use a different voice for when the toy was talking back to them.

One lady said, 'I am not sure what to do for the next Town Hall meeting.'

Toy: 'Why?'

Lady: 'Well, I don't want to repeat the same thing, because it would be boring.'

Toy: 'Why?'

Lady: 'We do the same thing every year, and colleagues are not engaged. I want to do something new, but I'm not sure what.'

Toy: 'Why?'

Lady (somewhat exasperated, perhaps): 'Because no one supports me, and I am worried they would laugh at the idea.'

Toy: 'Why?'

Lady: 'Oh ... actually, there's not much of a reason. It is just my worry.'

Soon enough, the room broke into laughter as people started having conversations with their toys. The "why" question gets annoying sometimes, but once you break through the annoying bits, the ideas come. The HR executive was inspired after talking to her toy. At some point she probably ignored the "why" questions and just kept rambling. The point is not what question the toy asked, but that the executive, using the toy as a channel, found a way to express herself. She stopped caring about others' judgments. She became playful herself. In the process she came to new ideas.

Peculiar as it may sound, by the end of a 10-minute conversation some people found solutions to their own problems through coaching themselves. Some were able to create distance between themselves and their personal challenges and were able to see them as less magnified. Therefore, they felt less stressed out.

All of them had a good laugh and felt more relaxed and reenergised.

During play, neurotrophins – chemicals in our brain – are produced. They encourage learning, improve emotional functioning, and reduce anxiety. Bill, who invited me to deliver the play session for his HR executives, affirmed my ideas: 'This is a different approach to managing stress, and makes it more fun, relaxing. We were also able to come up with creative solutions in the process and be reflective on our play histories, applying them to the management of our emotions at work. This also helped to stimulate conversation and enhance teamwork for long lasting effects, both personally and professionally.'

One HR manager wrote to me two days after the workshop.

*I have decided to use some of the playful things you taught us in the workshops for the Town Hall meeting – we will all be doing animal impressions.*

Another one contacted me a while later and told me that she had started asking her team to bring their toys to regular team meetings. They either used them as mascots, talked to toys like I had people do, or simply used them as springboards for conversations. This helped her colleagues get to know each other better.

Another time I brought in some plasticine, drawing paper, markers, and the snowflake toys that kids build with. I asked the executives to use the material to construct an image first of the type of leader they thought they were, and then of the type of leader they would like to become. In other words, they were asked to build their perceived selves and their ideal selves. This became the starting point of some interesting conversations about leadership. The difference and distance between the two constructions became metaphorical, demonstrating the development they needed go to through to become the leaders they wanted to be.

In one case, it became clear that the executive was already the leader he wanted to be, and yet his inner insecurities prevented him from seeing or accepting so. The executives marvelled at how playing helped them see themselves clearer; they enjoyed the therapeutic process of using their hands and

147

**Figure 35:** Who are you as a leader?

playing with toys once again. They thanked me profusely for teaching them how to play.

I found it curious that they thought I had "taught" them how to be playful. *Guiding* them to access their inner playfulness was perhaps more accurate. I do not think we need to be taught to be playful. But I do think we may need some inspiration and enabling to find daily playfulness for ourselves.

Think about what we used to love doing as children. We could spend the whole day without getting bored. For some, these activities might have been creative play with scraps of paper; for others it might have been imaginary play, running about in nature, playing with others, playing on one's own, reading a book …

Perhaps when people ask me "how" to play or "how" to use Bearapy, they are asking, 'How do I access my playfulness? How do I not feel embarrassed when I am playful? What is kind of play is appropriate?'

I cannot give prescribed answers, for they are different for everyone. However, here are some questions I thought it helpful to reflect upon:

1. In what way were you playful as a kid?

2. What could you do for ages and not get bored?

3. What did you play with? Why?

4. Who did you play with? Why?

5. How would you describe the feelings of play? How would you draw out those feelings?

6. How can you replicate these feelings today?

It would be valuable to think about our biases and assumptions about play as well, and reflect upon why we see playing the way we see it.

1. What do you consider play? What do you consider not to be play?

2. Why is something *not* play? Why do you think that? Who told you so?

3. When did you stop being playful?

4. What makes play unacceptable? Why?

What may be preventing you from playing today?

With another group of female executives in a multinational software company, we did exactly that. We drew. Our drawings didn't need to be renditions of Van Gogh – they just needed to be doodles and colours. And then we "made" play, with snowflake toys. Afterwards, we discussed what this meant for them. Slowly we were able to break through the preconceptions about play.

They learnt that they could be playful every day; they could think up stories in their heads on the way to the office, or find activities that would give them the same feeling they had when playing as a child. More importantly, they came to understand that playing stretches their minds and awareness. This awareness allows them to become more authentic leaders.

**Figure 36:** *What is play to you?*

The stories, the answers, are all in there in your head. And if you cannot think in the abstract, have a look at the toys around you, within your sight and within your reach.

1. Who gave you the object or toy?

2. Why do you like it / them?

3. What do you keep? What do you not keep?

4. If you have no toys, why not?

Create stories. You can have imaginary friends still. Build your best day with your son's blocks and figurines. What do you notice about how you feel in the process? There is a story to tell of every object around us. There is a chance for introspection, an opportunity to look around with curiosity, and a channel to express our stresses. These are novel ways through which HR practitioners, management, business owners, and entrepreneurs could help their staff relax. It takes a few minutes, and it's easily incorporated into everyday life – you can even do it walking down the corridor to the bathroom. Try to see how many colleagues you can get to smile at you as you pass by.

Playing is so easy, if only you allow yourself. Talk to your toys. Talk to your colleagues about your toys. Talk to your colleagues about their toys. Play with your food. Make objects with other objects. Playing with objects allows us to tell a story and to say things that are otherwise too difficult to put into words.

Listen to your own inner voice, and don't blindly adhere to society's preconceptions.

Even in creating Bearapy, I have been advised to be logical, have structure, identify the issue I want to solve, figure out who the target audience is, etc. That is all important – but then the structure prevents me from playing, imagining, listening to my own voice, and paying attention to my unconscious.

I played charades with the same group of HR executives, a game many of us have played before. The first step was to think of an animal. Then they stood in a circle and, one by one, they took it in turns to act like that animal. As they did this the rest of the group guessed which animal it was, and then they also had to act like the chosen creature. Cue hysterical laughter, especially when the animal depicted did not look like the animal at all. I could see the self-consciousness that goes with waving your arms and legs around in the air, as if they do not belong to you. There is always awkwardness, and you can tell that subconsciously people are pondering – *What if they can't guess the animal? What if I can't do it right?*

Right or wrong – according to who? We only put this judgment on ourselves. We run on biases and assumptions, and we don't even remember why we have them in the first place. So much depends on the approval and reactions of others.

Many women leaders have shared their anguish with me. They are oppressed by their façades. The pressure of having to have strength – and to be cool, calm, and collected, to relish in their roles of mother, leader, executive, boss, manager, employee, wife or daughter – caves in on them. The same is true for men. They have to answer to expectations. They feel a need to put bread on the table and excel in their roles as manager, husband, son, father, boss ... These overbearing duties crowd out playfulness. Many of us are on the brink of burnout and depression, without knowing it or being able to express it.

We have lost ourselves, not realising that a few seconds of play can reverse the burnout and build our resilience.

At the end of the same workshop with the hotel HR executives, I took the charades one step further. I asked the executives to think about how they felt for a few moments, d then invited them to express the feeling using an animal impression. Liberated from themselves, they loosened up, chortled with laughter, and extended their arms and legs and bodies to embrace the animal that represented how they felt: an eagle because they felt empowered, a turtle because they felt wise and grounded, a fish because they felt free in the water. This is just another way that people can be playful. A collective of playful individuals makes for effective group collaboration and a creative company culture. I can give you lots of research that shows the benefits of being playful, but I would like you to find what it means for *you* – not your boss, not your mother, not your neighbour.

As a start, here is one way. This is one thing I like doing whenever I feel stuck, bored, or stressed. It's a temporary relief: The Fish Face Impression. You must be thinking that that sounds easy, and yet it is so difficult to do that not many have been able to do one as fishy as mine. I started doing this impression in high school, and it has been the subject of ridicule, mocking, teasing, laughter, fun, and embarrassment all these years[82]. And it served to round people up. From colleagues to friends to classmates to professors, people have gathered together jovially to mimic me, and to enjoy moments of self-entertainment. More often than not, they break down laughing. The goal is not to do the perfect fish face – there is no goal, it is the fish face for the sake of doing the fish face.

If you are courageous enough to attempt the fish face, these are the steps:

1. Find a mirror

2. Close your lips and puff air up into your cheeks as much as possible

3. Then try to open and close your lips, keeping the puffed air in your cheeks

4. Increase the speed of opening and closing your lips

5. Do the fish face for 15 seconds without letting the air from your cheeks escape as you open and close your lips

6. Do the fish face with a colleague, a friend, a kid, or your boss. Do it together

7. Laugh and have fun

Go on! Try it!

**Figure 37:** *Dreamie.*
*Dreamie thinks life is a dream. He daydreams all day and lives in his candyfloss castle up in the clouds.*

# CHAPTER 15

# THE WORKPLACE

My work clothes used to be different shades of black, grey, white, and navy blue. There was no colour. I have heard descriptions of depression such as the "black dog", the "dark forest", the "unending night". But have you tried putting different colours of paint all together and mixing them? It becomes a blob of black. Black is a convergence of colours. Colours are *inside* the blackness. Colours are inside the darkness of depression. The art is to distil the different colours out, one by one, again. The skill is to look within for the individual colours.

The challenge is to see ourselves by studying the toys we treasure and the objects that adorn our environments, because that is where our hidden creativity and true colours lie.

As I recovered from depression and ventured into new career identities, I studied organisational psychology and merged my personal journey, academic research, and work experience to extend Bearapy into corporate and organisational settings. I looked at executives' and leaders' work desks, toys, and workspaces to find out how these faithful objects spur people on and relieve them of stress. In playing with individuals, I also saw how playfulness creates conversation and brings a group together. Playfulness is also central to company culture, especially in a day and age that nurtures creativity, innovation, and wellbeing.

Thus, a company that allows space for playfulness, makes way for a creative, healthy workplace.

Everyone likes to talk about creativity. Interior design is considered creative. And so, in order to add to this, companies could empower executives to personalise their workspace in order to develop their everyday creativity.

Without the academic gobbledegook, creativity involves two main aspects: "newness" and "problem-solving"[83]. Creativity is the production of new and useful ideas[84]. Everyday creativity is something we all have, if only we let ourselves embrace it[85]. Creativity comes in many guises: it could be coming up with another way to write an email response or making a shelf to prop up the computer screen for easier viewing. Everyday creativity in the work setting is about originality and meaningfulness[86], to find new solutions to existing problems, and to find new ways of thinking. Organisations are obsessed with creativity because it helps us keep up with societal and economic development. And yet they don't make the work environment conducive to creativity.

If companies included the element of playfulness into their culture and physical work space, employees would become healthier, more creative, and more productive. We don't need to think that all the walls of the offices need to be painted green or that the number of beanbags is directly proportional to staff's relaxation index or creativity quotient[87].

I know that some managers are concerned that play could distract from work, and the frequent worry is that it would be "unprofessional" and "immature." On the flip side, the cost of not playing could be depression and very grumpy, boring employees with their creativity suppressed.

Seemingly mindless actions like twirling a pen or fiddling with a puzzle toy do much more than just pass time. My good friend Andrew was the Asia-Pacific Head of Talent Management of a financial services firm. I chuckled when he told me he was bored on the regular late-night conference calls with Europe and the US – I was glad I did not have many of those. Sometimes his counterparts relied on him to fix problems from Asia. When not sure what to do or what new ideas to wow people with, Andrew would pick up the puzzle toy blocks on his work desk[88].

The blocks were a real-life metaphor for complex problem. Twirling, rotating, and stacking the blocks helped Andrew see things in a different light. The other side of his brain – the one that was not thinking about work issues in literal terms – was firing all sorts of neuron connections, helping his mind go into a problem-solving mode. The puzzles can be solved by swivelling the blocks into different configurations, and you can either follow the cards that come in the pack or move them in self-directed ways.

**Figure 38:** Andrew (42, male) plays with geometric puzzles when solving complex issues.

Andrew found that by playing with the puzzle, he was unconsciously thinking of solutions to business problems. Playing also made the calls less boring. Play and creativity are inextricably linked[89].

Play provides a culture of innovation. It encourages imagination and creativity at individual, group, and organisational levels[90] by stimulating divergent thinking and generating new ideas or novel associations between existing ideas[91]. The more I read about play, the more I see the significance of having senior executives be playful, for it fosters creative thinking[92].

Everyday creativity is exactly so: to contemplate the same issue from different angles. It helps you engineer new solutions and expose oneself to the possibilities of an ah-ha moment.

In office spaces it's mostly people's desks that have objects on them, and they enable play and creativity to prosper. Objects stand in silence on desks, but their messages are loud and bold – we just have not heard them. Some of the executives I have spoken to did not understand why they were emotionally attached to their objects. They simply interacted with them in different ways, playing silently and unknowingly. Whatever their small movements, they helped executives think. They helped them create. They helped them relax, de-stress, and find some fun and rejuvenation.

**Figure 39:** *A reminder to relax when faced with difficult issues at work (Vivian, 31, female).*

I once heard someone say in the office that they should not put stuffed animals on the desks because it wasn't professional, and only secretaries would do that to be "cute." The amount of unconscious bias contained in that phrase was humungous. We deadbolt ourselves to these lines of thought without questioning. Companies imitate, follow the herd, and install dartboards without considering the function and purpose of such things Architects, interior designers, scholars, executives and entrepreneurs deliberate about the work environment, wanting to create space that is conducive to creativity, team collaboration and relaxation. And yet, most of them focus mostly on open floor space, desk dimensions, ergonomics of swivel chairs, cushion colours, and incoherent pictures on the wall. The desks and workspaces – the places where employees spend most time – receive the least attention.

Desk spaces, cubicles, and offices are more than just physical locations. Desks are second homes to some people, and some want to decorate them with cathected objects, rather than designer items and curated paintings that mean nothing to them.

Having desktop objects represents a sense of belonging and loyalty to the organisation. Personal possessions, such as photos and mementos, mark personal territory and showcase

*Figure 40:* Beatrice (34, female) tidies her desk.

identity. In contrast, when people feel like their organisations are a temporary space for them and they intend to leave, they take less care to personalise their desks. One executive I spoke to even started to remove objects over the course of a few years as she became disheartened with the company[93].

As such, personalising the work desk and playing with objects has benefits for individual creativity and relaxation, but that is not all. The presence or absence of desktop objects reflects the organisational culture and the sense of belonging employees feel in the workplace[94]. Companies will do well to rethink the cliché of ping pong tables and allow employees to have toys and objects on their desks.

When I examined some organisations' work spaces, desktop objects provided a lens for me, through which I could get an idea of the company's culture. Most companies want their teams to be able to collaborate. Take the case of a start-up company I worked with here in Beijing. The tech team was overworked, they did not communicate with the sales team, and the office ambiance was tense. The founders were worried about the company culture and wanted the employees to have more fun. When I walked up to the office, I could immediately sense the stress. I went through the observations, the consulting, the recommendations. In the end we decided the priority was an informal space that meant something to the employees. We carved out a corner in the office space, got a cheap sofa, and then asked employees to bring something with which to decorate the space. Different toys showed up. Plants and books arrived. Slowly, people started to hang out around that space, chatting and asking each other about the toys. They also got to know each other better. Laughter started. The atmosphere defrosted.

It was that easy. These objects formed points of reference for building team relations.

Better team relations and more effective group cooperation also makes for less stressed out employees. Start-ups and entrepreneurial ventures make for interesting case studies on company culture. They are different beasts altogether from multinational companies. Studies[95] argue that entrepreneurs are 30% more likely to experience burnout and depression than their white-collar counterparts from large companies. Entrepreneurs put themselves, their identities, and their whole beings on the line to survive, to make something out of themselves, and to become the next big thing. Tech teams in start-ups like to work around the clock, getting into the flow when coding. Most employees are younger and do not mind the long hours. Indeed, most are expected to go the extra 10,000 miles just because it is a start-up. It is exhilarating to be part of building something from scratch.

Many of these young companies know to give perks like healthy snacks, gym memberships and flexible work times. What goes deeper though, is the mindset. Ouyang Yun, a good friend of mine who has started several companies in China, and is now President of a big internet company based in a number of countries in Asia, told me that the culture of working "9-9-6" (9am to 9pm, 6 days a week) is widely glorified but not sustainable. He learnt it the hard way too – after the first year of asking his employees to work on Saturdays, lots of them quit because they couldn't handle it anymore. So, the company scrapped that policy and Yun forced his tech team to go home earlier to be with their kids and families.

He told me that there is an upside to stress, and I agree. However, the issue is how people cope with the stress. Many office workers burn out not because of the quantity of the workload, but because the meaninglessness of their tasks make the work feel overwhelming. Yun ensures that everyone in his team understands how even the most trivial of tasks contribute to the overall strategy of the company's growth. That way, employees are driven and have a purpose. They no longer simply repeat the same motions every day in a stuffy office.

Yun himself is playful. He engages with his employees in a light-hearted way. He uses humour and creates a culture at work that embraces playfulness.

It may be less costly than most imagine. For employees who spend the bulk of their time in the office, company management can think about how to make the workspace more tenable so that employees feel a sense of belonging. They should consider providing a mental space where they can relax and cope with the stress, thus preventing the overwhelming sense of burnout. All it takes is to allow executives to keep some of their own toys on their desks, at zero cost to the company.

I have talked to many executives across Asia about the toys on their desks, and how the toys help them relax and de-stress on a busy work day[96]. It was curious to see that many played without knowing so. Many of them would reach out for the

 objects, touching, talking to, looking at, or playing with them. Some, like Zee, would rearrange the objects on the top of their desks regularly. Others would dust off the objects, or if their toys were broken, they would take immense effort to fix them.

**Figure 41:** Zee (26, female) rearranges her desktop objects regularly.

Yen manages a digital marketing agency in China. She told me that she often fixes toys on her windowsill that get broken when they're blown about by the wind. 'It keeps breaking. Either a leg will break or the tail will fall off, so I have to fix the funny horse.' Fixing the horse is therapeutic. It takes Yen's mind off the complexity of life for a while and refreshes her, allowing her to revisit her task at hand[97].

Some people I met through Bearapy multitasked, performing activities at the same time as engaging with their toys, such as staring at postcards stuck on the cubicle wall, flicking a pen back and forth, or swinging a pendulum. A business executive told me that half the time she doesn't realise that she's turning a model of a mini globe on her desk as she is thinking, and in some mysterious way, playing with the mini global model helped her think.

*Figure 42:* Yen (42, female) fixes toys broken by the wind.

Companies have a responsibility to their employees and it's in their best interests to keep them emotionally and mentally fit – it maximises performance, increases productivity, and contributes to the company's bottom line. In turn, the company can exceed stakeholders' expectations and ensure a secure work environment and job security for employees.

However, the responsibility doesn't just lie with companies. Employees themselves should open up to the ideas of stress management, playfulness, and becoming more self-aware. Executives are the ones who need to find the audacity to face themselves, their individual fears, and their hidden emotions. They should have the courage to be vulnerable through playfulness.

We already know how to play. Instead of looking outwards for tips to boost creativity, we need to turn inwards and look at what we have readily on our desks. We need to tap into our inner children. Organisations don't need to purchase expensive equipment: they just need to encourage executives to play with something that means something to them. That's when their creativity will flourish.

Judge not your managers by the fluffy pencil cases on their desks – they could well be the remedy to business problems.

Play does not need to take up a bulk of scheduled time – it could be incorporated into our daily lives and during work hours. Even if you only engage with it for a few minutes, a playful attitude could go a long way. It enhances your performance, reinforces productivity, creates employee engagement, helps you adapt to changes and cements corporate culture.

Playfulness unearths the hidden colours within us, the same way we can extract the different colours from a blob of black paint. Play positively impacts health and wellbeing by relieving stress, building social bonds, and inspiring creativity.

After my recovery from depression, my wardrobe changed. Now it features different shades, tones, saturations and brightness. I have garments that are highlighter yellow and magenta pink, royal purple and coral turquoise.

Your colours are there. Only your own mind shields them from you.

**Figure 43:** Lotie.
*Lotie sits on a lotus leaf in the Culture Corner. She is highly intellectual but does not have much self-confidence. She is in a fragile state of being and is trying to recreate her identity. She needs time to nurture and be kind to herself. She is crummie's friend because they both see life differently and have perspectives of their own. Conformity is not an option.*

# CHAPTER 16

# THE WORKPLACE

We are employees, bosses, friends, wives, husbands, siblings. We have been someone else's children. And many of us have, or will have, children.

I was crushed listening to Jojo's story. She was in senior management in an oil and gas company here in Beijing. She was trilingual, softly spoken but with presence, and well-travelled. She was about to get another promotion within her company.

She loved drawing cartoons, and on her desk in the office were doodles she had done in between meetings and the hustle and bustle of work. She told me how her mother nags her to stop drawing cartoons, even now that she is 40 years old and has become a mother herself. Her mother pesters her to take her daughter to extra mathematics tutorial classes. Maybe she could be a physicist one day – win a Nobel Prize, even!

Jojo was stressed at work and stressed at home. Her parents, children, husband, team and boss all depended on her. She had no time to break down.

I was surprised at how she was still controlled by the older generation, though perhaps it is not so astounding after all. The idea of respecting our elders has been taken to the extreme.

It is sandwiched by feelings of guilt. How often have we heard, 'If you do not listen, you are therefore a bad child! And look at everything your parents have sacrificed for you! They did not have such opportunities.'

As parents, we vow not to do the same to our children. But, uncontrollably and inevitably, some of us repeat the same patterns, suffocating our children. It is a game (excuse the pun) of keeping up with the Wangs, the Lis and the Jones. *His son is doing kung fu, charcoal drawing, the trumpet and swimming classes – and so must mine!* Whether our kids enjoy these activities is not of concern.

Playing somehow has a bad reputation. Some trauma must be inhibiting our parents, stopping them from expressing their playfulness. My Korean neighbour came to our apartment one day, distressed and irritated. She had made a complaint to management and was now complaining directly to us. This neighbour lived below us, and my daughter often ran from her bedroom, down the corridor and into the living room. The neighbour found it a nuisance to hear the footsteps pattering.

'Children should not play at home,' she said to me. 'Home is for relaxing only!'

I didn't know how to respond. I was flabbergasted. If my children couldn't play at home of all places, where else could they play? In fact, I wish they could play everywhere, all the time, for the sake of their own health. If home cannot be a refuge where my kids can play and be themselves, then I have failed immensely as a parent.

As parents we unknowingly shape our kids. What are the restrictions we are creating for our children? And what experiences do we leave them with? We are all made up of our pasts.

Shana, an HR executive I met, bought five stones (a game she played with as a child). The stones come in little bags, and she played with them on a whim because they reminded her of her childhood[98].

Others' stories were not so fun. Nancy, a Japanese female executive, told me a heartbreaking story[99]. She loved dolls and had many of them as a child. As an adult, she sometimes feels she needs to "graduate" from having dolls. Almost in tears, she stuttered through her memories of being in the fifth grade. She had a kingdom of stuffed animals, a corner of

*Figure 44: Nancy's (40, female) beloved bear on her desk.*

paradise in an imaginary world. But her mother got worried about her and destroyed her world, throwing out all of her stuffed animals one day while she was at school. When Nancy came home, she was shocked. She's been traumatised by it since.

*Figure 45: Shana (43, female) played five stones as a child.*

This harrowing episode hurt her so much that 30 years later it still affected her behaviour. Nancy was attached to a yellow bear on her work desk, but she now seemed ashamed of having the bear there for it was not "grown up." And yet she couldn't throw it away. She mended the bear with threads when it fell apart and couldn't sit properly. She had a love-hate relationship with the bear, because it reminded her of her heartbreak growing up. As an adult she was rejecting her inner child because the woman who loved her the most also hurt her the most.

As a parent now myself, I wonder – how do I unknowingly inhibit my children's creativity? I am part of an online group chat for parents who want to exchange ideas on helping their children be creative. At first the amount of parental interference was alarming. The attachment to courses that "teach" kids "how" to play, use bricks, and follow instructions reflected parents' fear of not being good enough. The group chat's objective – giving kids the opportunity to play – was ironic, because all that the parents discussed was how to limit their free play with instructions, specific toys, and ways to build robots. Why could we not simply give kids their bricks and see what they do with them? What about toilet rolls and scraps of paper, aluminium foil and glue? Why couldn't we see what the children made out of them?

One conversation in the group chat went as follows:

'I would like to attend this play course too!'

'Well, then you have to be five and a half years old again.'

The assumption was that adults cannot play, or that indeed there were no "play classes" for adults. It aggravates me to witness this shallowness. Pre-nursery playgroups that focus on teaching skills – such as constructing the perfect cotton ball ice cream cone – suffocate children from the beginning. Free play fosters the creative mind. Playful children become playful teenagers, who are more mentally resilient, emotionally aware, and able to achieve better examination results[100].

I get it, as a parent of two munchkins. We want the best for them. Inadvertently, we deplete them of their individual minds and unique ways to view the world. Many would attribute adulthood issues and psychological problems to childhood trauma, or the deprivation of love and care. *The Book of Life* – an offshoot of the organisation The School of Life – alerts us to the Golden Child Syndrome: "we may wind up mentally unwell, not so much because we were ignored or maltreated, but because we were loved with a distinctive and troubling over-intensity, because we were praised for capacities that we did not possess and could not identify with and because we were asked – with apparent kindness but underlying unwitting manipulation – to shoulder the hopes and longings of our carers rather than our own deep selves."[101]

We declare our children as geniuses and want to give them the best. So we suffocate them with courses and playgroups to learn how to build blocks. It is a superfluous and commercial ploy.

Give children blocks and let them decide what to do with them, instead of getting them to "play properly." Children then look to us to approve of the structures they build, and we praise them for every little move. This makes them believe that they have a "latent fraudulence and a consistent fear that it will be unmasked."[102] I was one of these Golden Child Tiger Cubs. I had impostor syndrome as I entered the workforce. I had been told I was special, with a uniqueness I could not identify with or see the grounds for. I was taught to play right, play properly, follow the rules, and then to stop playing.

I have a plea to parents: leave children be, or they will follow in my steps on the path of self-destruction. Try not to create frameworks and encourage the pursuit of success and achievement right from infancy. I remind myself of this everyday as a parent. I often re-read this letter I wrote to my daughter and to myself[103]:

*Dearest Riviane,*

*You are enough.*

*Do not let anyone – especially me – ever doubt you.*

*Live for yourself and not to anyone's expectations – not society's, not your parents', not your grandparents', not your friends'. There is no image you need to live up to.*

*Seek help when you need; you do not have to be strong all the time.*

*Cry, scream, whine, throw tantrums. Express your frustrations, your anger, and your jealousies all you need. It frees up space for giggles, laughter, fun, love, joy, and hope.*

*Giggle. Giggle at the simplest things like blowing raspberries at Arlie in the bathtub.*

*Do not suppress your emotions. Have people around you who let you express how you feel without telling you how you "should" or "should not" feel.*

*If you do not enjoy something, do not force yourself to "enjoy the moment."*

*Have the courage to play, to talk to yourself, to sing to yourself, and to have a conversation with your toys.*

*Playing and daydreaming does more to a healthy life than any knowledge you stuff into your brain, so refuse my attempts to force you to memorise vocabulary or multiplication tables.*

*You do not need anyone to tell you that you are beautiful and intelligent. You are. You know that. That's that.*

*Be your own person. No one owns you. You are not "my" baby; you are not anyone's treasure. You are you.*

*There are people in this world less blessed than you – but this is not a reason to not have the sorrows or worries that you feel.*

*I will unknowingly project my fears onto you, try to live vicariously through you, and endeavour to protect you from the heartache and pain I had when I was growing up. Give them back to me, because you are you, and you will experience life in your own way.*

*I apologise in advance for all the mistakes I make and all the things I said I would do but forget to. I am sorry for my tantrums and words that will hurt you. I have my own shit to deal with and I am learning. Teach me.*

*I try not to be the mother or wife I said I would not be, but it is not always a smooth ride. You have every right to tell me to go look at myself.*

*Build up your husband / wife / partner; do not tear him / her down or question him / her endlessly like I do. Let him / her be forever your soulmate.*

*You will have mentors and teachers. You will hear many words of wisdom from others, and guidance from all over the world. You do not have to follow everything they say.*

*Make up your own mind. Concoct your own wisdom.*

*Have a mission and a vision for yourself, but you do not always need to know where you are going. Scattered confusion is just as fun.*

*Help others when you can.*

*You will find things unfair. Life is unfair. Maybe you will be the one to change the world. Trust in your inner light.*

*Be kind to yourself. Be kind to animals and to plants.*

*Jump, hop, skip, dance, roll on the grass, and do cartwheels.*

*Listen to yourself, your body, your heart, your brain, your mind, your stomach.*

*I believe in your beliefs and dreams. You might be the only one swimming southeast while everyone else is going north. I hope you find the strength in the alone-ness and in forging new grounds. The world is waiting to hear your story too.*

*Ignore fuzzy wuzzy quotes on social media, such as how the night is darkest before dawn. They fuel other people's insecurities to make themselves feel better. There will be storms, thunder and lightning. There will be miserable days and funk times. By all means, feel miserable and funky all you need, instead of forcing a smile.*

*They (whoever they are) say I need to be the role model for you. I am afraid that is tough for me. It stresses me out to know you look up to me, because I am still learning to love myself for who I am. But perhaps I could be the anti-role model – you could see in me the behaviours you do not want to repeat. Mothers are not always right.*

*Even though I think something might be good for you, it might not be so. I could be wrong. Help me realise that.*

*Keep the twinkle in your big eyes. Disappointments will make you cry. One day you will grow weary too. This is part of life.*

*Think positively, think negatively, and everything in between.*

*Do not waste time trying to overcome fears. Greet them, embrace them, talk to them, know them, and befriend them.*

*When everyone is busy making New Year resolutions, go and play. Calendars are but a temporal mark of time. Each day is a day. Let not months or years inhibit you with frameworks of time or pressure you into achieving "Goals for 2027".*

*If you fall, and do not want to get up, I will lie next to you and be with you – and I will keep quiet.*

*You are good enough. Always.*

*Love,*

*Nochie*

We overwhelm children with things to do and instructions on what not to do. So often, we are not aware of imposing our own biases and preconceptions onto them. We need to ask ourselves, 'Why are we asking our children to *learn* how to play with blocks?' Instead of giving them aims and objectives, simply allow them to play. I have had parents ask me how to play with their kids. I would say to simply be present and next to them and let them lead. Let them show you how they want you to play with them.

They will learn what they will learn. Kids will play. It may do us adults well to learn from them to play more – to have the same curiosity to explore, imagine, and wonder.

Let children *be*.

**Figure 46:** *Babie.*
*The smallest and youngest of all the bears, Babie is silly and whiny. He lives up to his name. In fact, he is curious about everything, has an imaginative and creative mind, and constantly protects his inner child from the world's contamination. It is not the age that matters – it is the attitude.*

# CHAPTER 17

# INNER CHILD

Play is not a specific activity, and it is not just about toys. It is an approach to life, a curiosity, a contemplation. Parents woulddo well to play more. Companies would do well to allow employees to be more playful and give them a mental and physical space to do so. All these things will lead to healthier individuals.

I acknowledge that stress can come from everywhere, especially in this day and age – and especially in life in the city. Today's demands are tremendous, the expectations are real, and the competition is fierce. Mental health issues such as depression and burnout are real. They can hit anyone, big or small, tall or short, young or old, corporate or not.

We can thrive in corporate jobs, or in any job for that matter. But we must understand ourselves first. It's good to be open to exploring your inner self, knowing that there are some things about yourself that you might not know. Finding your playful self gives you the courage to be vulnerable and the ability to cope with stress in novel, creative ways. Indeed, playful people find fewer situations stressful!

In play, I allow myself to be kind to myself for a few seconds. I release myself from self-imposed pressure. I stop being harsh to myself, because whenever I am anything less than super perfect it feeds my internal sense of inadequacy.

I like my fish faces and animal impressions. I love my bears and my doodles. I delight in being silly. I amuse myself with comparing how my daughter looks to cartoon characters. I take photos of her hair and facial expressions and make photo collages of her next to pictures of Lucky Trolls or Tweety Bird. I revel in how alike they look, because both of those things were my favourite back in school days. I work with objects, with toys, with lumps of fake poo. I am playful. That is who I am.

Be bold and express your playful nature. Be childlike, so that your inner child can live together in harmony with your adult self.

Through play we can dismantle the scaffolding of professionalism. We can stop pushing ourselves to live in ways we think are expected of us. We can dissolve our vanity and pride in material goods, so that we can be at peace with ourselves.

And there is no huge cost. It is FREE for everyone.

Take the first step towards being playful: do the fish face!

**Figure 47:** *Gurie.*
*Gurie is a wise, sagacious bear. He meditates. He is zen all the time. Gurie is well-read in comparative philosophy and psychology. He imparts bear wisdom to those who seek inner peace and serenity.*

# EPILOGUE OF BEING

For one last time before I left Tokyo for Beijing almost a decade ago, I savoured the last chance for *Hanami*. Hana means "flowers", and mi means "to look" in Japanese. It was a revered festive fortnight-long celebration to appreciate the ephemeral beauty of the sakura, the unique flower with cherry blossoms for which Japan is famous. It is a custom to gather with friends at parks, sitting down with an abundance of alcohol and bento boxes of sushi under the budding flowers. The sakura is in bloom for only a few weeks a year during spring, and the Japan Meteorological Agency makes accurate predictions early on in the year, detailing which parts of Japan will see these fleeting flowers and at which times.

I went to as many picnics as I could fit in with Timmie. The cherry blossom trees seemed to be giving me a warning with their intertwined branches: *cherish the laughter around you and treasure the carefree time you spend with your friends. Nothing is permanent, and you will not be an energetic and omnipotent young adult forever.* There would come a time when I would not see anyone for months.

Of course, I paid no attention to the solemn message the transitory sakura was sending me.

I remember the eerie sense of nostalgia I felt as I romped around on the grass with my friends, making funny faces into the cameras during Hanami. I drank *ume-shu,* my favourite plum wine, and flitted among people from noon till sunset under the shade of the flowers. I swept away the fallen petals and the caution they whispered into my ears.

The Japanese sakura petals were soon replaced with frosty Beijing snowflakes. They were beautiful, like soft powder, but the build-up couldn't be safe. Unassuming, the snow gathered calmly. It reflected the scorching sunlight. I blinked, and I blinked again.

The snow built up and built up – and then the earth trembled and shuddered. There was a crash, and the avalanche of depression overpowered me.

Depression was a blinding light. It was so bright, so clear, so white, as if angels in all their glory had descended upon my bubble of ignorance and arrogance. They were there to tell me to live again, simply, as myself. It gave me a sudden clarity. I was not who I thought I was. I was lost. I saw so clearly that I was lost.

The move from Tokyo to Beijing was, in my mind, the next step up. In reality, it brought me down into a snowy hell, where I found myself once again. I reconfigured, I played, I dreamt.

But it was not the end. I recovered. I found a harmony in my new career and in being myself. As I put myself together, I found meaning for work. And now I have a life.

Balance is overrated, because it suggests that we can fairly divide up our time and energy for all the different parts of our lives. I prefer finding harmony, because it means we find a mixture that is suitable for ourselves and appropriate for the amount of time we have. We can blend in all the elements and obligations and passions and responsibilities of life.

As strange as it sounds to most people, I wish I could go back to depression. I wish I had better understood the messages it gave me.

Most people scoff at me when I say I wish I'd experienced my depression more deeply, stayed with the emotions. For most, it is imperative to "get out of it" as soon as possible. To return to "normal." But what is normal?

We focus too much on the triggers for our depression (work stress, traumatic events, hormones?) and we focus too little on the deeper meaning of it. We are quick to offer solutions, but neglect to understand the people who are depressed. We want to lift their spirits so that we feel more comfortable around them. We are quick to find ways to limit the "bad" characteristics associated with depression – laziness, disinterest, lack of motivation, aggression, tardiness – because they stop people from becoming the type of employees that climb the corporate ladder and stay on the top rungs.

Depression is a message for individuals, families, companies and organisations that something needs to change. It's a message most of us choose to ignore, because it is easier to do away with the pain on the surface level, and then pretend everything is okay again – that we are one happy family, that we are fulfilled individuals, that our companies are doing something right because there are free snacks and ping pong tables.

I am long past the debilitating years where I could not perform even the simplest function, such as getting out of bed, putting clothes on and walking from the bedroom to the living room. I have built a new career, a company, and a social cause based on my personal experience. But depression has not left me; it is part of me, and it visits me from time to time. I have gone through episodes again and again, especially after the birth of my two children. I went into the loops of rumination. I convinced myself that my life was an asinine vacuum, worth nothing to anyone – especially when I encountered endless rejections and ridicule when pioneering playfulness, the very foundation of my company. In every step of The Struggle, a term coined by the well-known investor Ben Horowitz[104], I was apprehensive of whether I would get through.

Each time I felt incapacitated. Each time I savoured the moroseness. When I felt a sense of doom, it opened up the space for me to excavate my unconscious thoughts and unearth what depression was trying to tell me about myself.

Today, I live for myself. I find myself in play.

Through depression, I saw a kaleidoscope of possibilities.

Thank you, Depression.

**Figure 48:** *Proudie.*
*Proudie is proud and encouraging of every trivial result that anyone or any bear achieves. He finds solace with Shinie and Happie, as they muse about the wonders of life and accomplishments humans have made.*

## ACKNOWLEDGEMENTS

I would like to express my utmost gratitude to the team at Trigger, particularly to Stephanie Cox and Katie Taylor for their guidance in editing the manuscript, James Waller and Hannah Abrahaley for their patience and enthusiasm in setting a vision for my book, and Elise Jackson for her support in making sure my book is read by people around the world, so that we can help more people. I would also like to thank my publicist, Claire Maxwell, for her expertise in sharing my book with a wide audience.

My sincere thanks to those who were willing to support me through endorsing this book, and for the taking the time to read and make suggestions: Chris Underhill MBE for mentoring my quest and taking me under his wing; Vivian Lau for opening up opportunities for me; Rui Ma for being inspirational in her work in transformative tech and mental health; Kai-Ming Cheng for guiding my long-winding road since my university days; and Bill Lu for playing devil's advocate for a lot of my crazy Bearapy ideas. I would also like to thank everyone else who has provided an endorsement for *Stress and the City*.

I am in debt to those who have supported the development of Bearapy throughout the years: the Program Directors for the Executive Masters in Coaching and Consulting for Change at INSEAD; Professor Roger Lehman and Professor Erik van de Loo; Susan Tang, our course coordinator and one of my early supporters; classmates and alumni at INSEAD; friends who let me experiment at their companies and start-up firms, and the first clients who took a risk on me. Also, I am most thankful to those who agreed to let me use their experiences and reflections in my research and publication of the findings in my thesis and in this book.

A lot of bear hugs to Dai Cameron, the designer for all the Bearapy campaign pictures in the chapter "Awareness," who has long been a great friend of me and my husband's and who graciously offered his designs and sketches for free for Bearapy to use in pursuing its cause.

I express my deepest gratitude to Dr Stephen-Claude Hyatt, without whom I would not still be alive, for being my therapist for some seven years and now my supervisor as I continue on this work. Without his guidance, support, therapy, cajoling, unconditional trust, confidence in my abilities and a knock on the head when I needed one, Bearapy would not be what it is today.

Bearapy and Enoch could thrive only because we have a group of close friends who did not hesitate to give brutal comments when needed, and who offered lots of love and support in my journey, especially when I got derailed. In no particular order, all my love to: Sarah Lo, Betty Ng, Sarah Matsushita, Scarlet So, Vienna Fong, Xavier Yeung, Gary Cheng, Paul Harvey, Camila Renault Falcao, Alexander Shapiro, Birgitta Leopold, Anika Saggar, Elaine Yu, Eugene Tang, Winnie Wong, Katja Wiegratz, Mavis McAllister, Yi Liu, Oma Lee, and Wang *laoshi*, my calligraphy teacher. Thank you for staying with me, accepting me for who I am, giving me confidence and encouragement when I was in dire need of it, and trusting that I would one day get this book written.

The Bears have a special place in my heart of course, and without a doubt they have played a key part in Bearapy's invention. Most of all, I thank Floppie for showing up with smiles every single second.

Last but not least, all my love to my husband, Timothy Coghlan, for taking our kids, Riviane Jade and Arlen Jade, to Australia for a month so that I could have the peace and quiet to write this book. And also, needless to say, for sticking it out through thick and thin all these years, throughout my depressive episodes, suicide attempts, temper tantrums, days of rotting, and just for lying there with me.

Thank you to everyone for making my childhood dream of writing a book a reality.

# If you found this book interesting ...
## why not read this next?

# Stripped Bare

## Swapping Credit for Compassion

*Stripped Bare* is an eye-opening, stigma busting, inspiring tale that shines a light on the toxic effects of consumerism within today's society.

**If you found this book interesting ...
why not read this next?**

# Depression in a Digital Age

## The Highs and Lows of Perfectionism

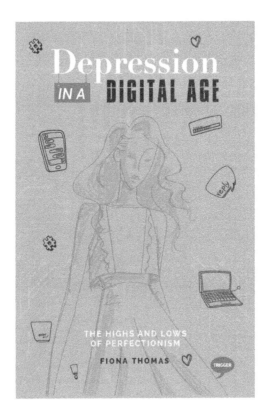

*Depression in a Digital Age* traces the journey of a young woman's search for perfection in a world filled with filters.

**If you found this book interesting ...**
**why not read this next?**

## Shiny Happy Person

### Finding the Sun Between Clouds of Depression

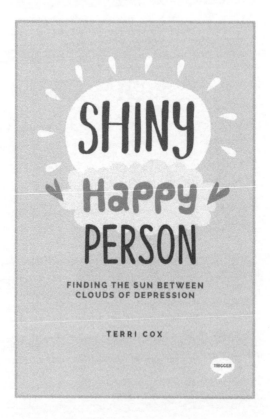

*Shiny Happy Person* is the story of one girl's inspirational rise after a devastating mental breakdown that gave her tormenting panic attacks, suicidal thoughts, bouts of insomnia and crippling headaches.

# REFERENCES

**THE OVERACHIEVER**

1 **Carroll, L.** (1865). *Alice's Adventures in Wonderland.* New York: D. Appleton & Company.

**IMPOSTOR**

2 **The American Institute of Stress.** Retrieved from www.stress.org/workplace-stress/

3 These losses can be quantified at the population level by multiplying the prevalence of these disorders by the average level of disability associated with them, to give estimates of years lived with disability. **World Health Organization** (2017). *Depression and Other Common Mental Disorders: Global Health Estimates,* WHO/MSD/MER/2017.2. Retrieved from www.who.int/mental_health/management/depression/ prevalence_global_health_estimates/en/Estimate report

4 **World Health Organization.** *Metrics: Disability-adjusted life year.* Retrieved from www.who.int/healthinfo/ global_burden_disease/metrics_daly/en/

5 **Prüss-Ustün, A., Wolf, J., Corvalán, C., Bos, R., & Neira, M.** (2016). *Preventing disease through healthy environments: a global assessment of the burden of disease from environmental risks.* Switzerland: World Health Organization. Retrieved from www.who.int/quantifying_ehimpacts/publications/ en/9241546204chap3.pdf

**6  World Health Organization.** *Disability weights, discounting and age weighting of DALYs.* Retrieved from www.who.int/healthinfo/global_burden_disease/daly_disability_weight/en/

**7  World Health Organization.** *Depression: Key facts.* Retrieved from www.who.int/news-room/fact-sheets/detail/depression

**8  Prüss-Ustün, A., Wolf, J., Corvalán, C., Bos, R., & Neira, M.** (2016). *Preventing disease through healthy environments: a global assessment of the burden of disease from environmental risks.* Switzerland: World Health Organization. Retrieved from www.who.int/quantifying_ehimpacts/publications/en/9241546204chap3.pdf

**INVINCIBLE**

**9  Wikipedia.** Retrieved from https://en.wikipedia.org/wiki/Migraine

**DEFRAGMENTATION**

**10 World Health Organization** (2017). *Depression and Other Common Mental Disorders: Global Health Estimates,* WHO/MSD/MER/2017.2. Retrieved from www.who.int/mental_health/management/depression/prevalence_global_health_estimates/en/

**11 World Health Organization** (2017). *Depression and Other Common Mental Disorders: Global Health Estimates,* WHO/MSD/MER/2017.2. Retrieved from www.who.int/mental_health/management/depression/prevalence_global_health_estimates/en/

**SUPER PERFECT**

**12 Chua, A.** (2011). *Battle Hymn of the Tiger Mother.* US: Penguin.

**13 Miller, A.** (1997). *The Drama of the Gifted Child: The Search for the True Self (revised edition).* US: Basic Books.

**14 BBC** (2011, January 22). Are strict Chinese mothers the best? Retrieved from www.bbc.com/news/magazine-12249215

**15 James, O.** (2008). *Affluenza.* UK: Random House.

**16 BBC** (2011, January 22). Are strict Chinese mothers the best? Retrieved from www.bbc.com/news/magazine-12249215

**17 Pop News** (2017, April 18). Retrieved from www.popnews.hk/?p=17591

**18 Pappas, S.** (2012, January 19). Study: 'Tiger Parenting' Tough on Kids. *Live Science.* Retrieved from www.livescience.com/18 023-tiger-parenting-tough-kids.html

**19 Pappas, S.** (2011, June 24). Why Everyone's a Parenting Expert. *Live Science.* Retrieved from www.livescience.com/ 14774-judgmental-parent-insecurity.html

**20 Rettner, R.** (2009, Aug 4). We Learn More from Success than Failure. *Live Science.* Retrieved from www.livescience.com/ 10559-learn-success-failure.html

## BURNOUT

**21 Bloom, D., Cafiero, E., Jané-Llopis, E., Abrahams-Gessel, S., Bloom, L., Fathima, S., et al.** (2011). *The Global Economic Burden of Non-communicable Diseases.* Geneva: World Economic Forum.

**22 Beyond Blue** (2014), *State of Workplace Mental Health in Australia.* This comprises $4.7 billion in absenteeism, $6.1 billion in presenteeism and $146 million in compensation claims. Retrieved from www.headsup.org.au/ docs/default-source/resources/bl1270-report---tns-the-state-of-mental-health-in-australian-workplaces-hr.pdf?sfvrsn=8

**23 Grove, B.** (2009). Mental health in the workplace. *Occupational Health,* 61(2), 36-39.

**24 NAMI.** (2015). *Bad for Business: The Business Case for Overcoming Mental Illness Stigma in the Workplace.* Massachusetts: National Alliance on Mental Illness of Massachusetts.

**25 The Shaw Mind Foundation.** *Mental health and business: The cost of mental health and ways to reduce the impact on business.* UK: The Shaw Mind Foundation. Retrieved from http://shawmindfoundation.org/wp-content/uploads /2016/04/Shaw-Mind-Guide-to-Cost-to-business.pdf

**26 Frey, J.J.** (2014). Why Employers Must Help Stop Suicide. *Insurancethoughtleadership.com, September 17.* Retrieved from http://insurancethoughtleadership.com/why-employers-must-help-stop-suicide.

**27 World Economic Forum** (2012). *The Workplace Wellness Alliance: Investing in a Sustainable Workforce.* Retrieved from http://image-src.bcg.com/Images/The_Workplace_Wellness_ Alliance_Jan_2012_tcm9-105947.pdf

**28 World Economic Forum** (2010). *The New Discipline of Workforce Wellness: Enhancing Corporate Performance by Tackling Chronic Disease.* Geneva: World Economic Forum.

**29 The Shaw Mind Foundation.** *Mental health and business: The cost of mental health and ways to reduce the impact on business.* UK: The Shaw Mind Foundation.

**30 World Economic Forum** (2012). *The Workplace Wellness Alliance: Investing in a Sustainable Workforce.* Retrieved from http://image-src.bcg.com/Images/The_Workplace_Wellness_ Alliance_Jan_2012_tcm9-105947.pdf

**HUGS**

**31 Noch Noch.** (2011, March 1). *The partner in this whole ordeal.* Retrieved from http://nochnoch.com/2011/03/01/the-partner-in-this-whole-ordeal/

**32 Noch Noch.** (2012, February 20). *10 things not to say to a depressed person (and please don't ever say to me either).* Retrieved from http://nochnoch.com/2012/02/20/10-things-not-to-say-to-a-depressed-person-and-please-dont-ever-say-to-me-either/

33 **Noch Noch.** (2012, February 20). *10 things to say or to do with a depressed person.* Retrieved from http://nochnoch. com/2013/06/17/10-things-to-say-to-or-do-with-a-depressed-person/

**THE MAGIC**

34 **Dr Seuss.** Retrieved from www.aboutdays.com/quotes/dr-seuss-adults-are-just-outdated-children--1152.html#gsc. tab=0

**BEARAPY**

35 **Liao, J.** His works can be found at http://www.jimmyspa.com.

36 **Styhre, A.** (2008). The Element of Play in Innovation Work: The Case of New Drug Development. *Creativity and Innovation Management,* 17(2), 136–46.

37 **Barlow, M.R.C., DeMarni Caron, L., Freyd, H.P., & Jennifer, J.** (2012). Comparison of Normative and Diagnosed Dissociation on Attachment to Companion Animals and Stuffed Animals. *Psychological Trauma: Theory, Research, Practice,and Policy,* 4(5), 501-06.

38 **Winnicott, D. W.** [1971] (2005). *Playing and Reality* (2nd ed.). USA & Canada: Routledge.

39 **Winnicott, D. W.** [1971] (2005). *Playing and Reality* (2nd ed.). USA & Canada: Routledge.

40 **Freud, S.** [1911] (1958). Formulations on the Two Principles of Mental Functioning. *The Standard Edition of the Complete Psychological Works of Sigmund Freud XII* (pp.218-26). London: Hogarth Press.

41 **Winnicott, D. W.** [1971] (2005). *Playing and Reality* (2nd ed.). USA & Canada: Routledge.

42 **Bollas, C.** (1987). *The Shadow of the Object: Psychoanalysis of the Unthought Known.* New York: Columbia University Press.

**43 Lee, A.** Ambrose no longer has a retail store, but you can contact him or visit his warehouse. Facebook: www.facebook.com/profile.php?id=769349368; Instagram: @ambrosele; WeChat: toymuseum.

**44 Li, N.N.** (2016, May 4). Vitamin play. *AsiaSpa*. Retrieved from www.asiaspa.com/10425/vitamin-play/

**45 Li, N.N.** (2016, May 4). Vitamin play. *AsiaSpa*. Retrieved from www.asiaspa.com/10425/vitamin-play/

**46 Li, E.** (2015). *Desktop Playground: Transitional objects at play for everyday creativity in the workplace* (Executive Masters Thesis). INSEAD, Singapore.

**47 Li, E.** (2015). *Desktop Playground: Transitional objects at play for everyday creativity in the workplace* (Executive Masters Thesis). INSEAD, Singapore.

**48 Li, E.** (2015). *Desktop Playground: Transitional objects at play for everyday creativity in the workplace* (Executive Masters Thesis). INSEAD, Singapore.

**49 Winnicott, D. W.** [1971] (2005). *Playing and Reality* (2nd ed.). USA & Canada: Routledge.

**PLAY**

**50 Huizinga, J.** (1971). *Homo Ludens: A Study of the Play-Element in Culture.* Boston: Beacon Press.

**51 Sutton-Smith, B.** (2001). *The Ambiguity of Play.* Massachusetts: Harvard University Press.

**52 Li, N.N.** (2016, May 4). Vitamin play. *AsiaSpa*. Retrieved from www.asiaspa.com/10425/vitamin-play/

**53 Gordon, G.** (2014). Well Played: The Origins and Future of Playfulness. *American Journal of Play*, 6(2), 234–66. Retrieved from www.journalofplay.org/

**54 Glynn, M.A., & Webster, J.** (1992). The Adult Playfulness scale: An Initial Assessment. *Psychological Reports*, 71, 83–103.

**55 Li, N.N.** (2016, May 4). Vitamin play. *AsiaSpa*. Retrieved from www.asiaspa.com/10425/vitamin-play/

**56 de Koven, B.** (2014). *A Playful Path*. Retrieved from Lulu.com

**57 de Koven, B.** (2015). *The Politics of Playfulness*. TEDxAsheville. Retrieved from https://youtu.be/FnG3-k5phUM

**58 Li, E.** (2015). *Desktop Playground: Transitional objects at play for everyday creativity in the workplace* (Executive Masters Thesis). INSEAD, Singapore.

**59 Li, E.** (2015). *Desktop Playground: Transitional objects at play for everyday creativity in the workplace* (Executive Masters Thesis). INSEAD, Singapore.

**60 Li, E.** (2015). *Desktop Playground: Transitional objects at play for everyday creativity in the workplace* (Executive Masters Thesis). INSEAD, Singapore.

**61 Klein, K.E.** (2014, March). Too distracted to work: The dark side of open offices. *Business Week,* March 13, 3.

**Maxwell, S., Reed, G., Saker, J., & Story, V.** (2005). The two faces of playfulness: A new tool to select potentially successful sales reps. *Journal of Personal Selling & Sales Management, XXV*(3), 215–29.

**Ofori-Dankwa, J., & Julian, S.D.** (2004). Conceptualizing social science paradoxes using the diversity and similarity curves model: Illustrations from the work/play and theory novelty/continuity paradoxes. *Human Relations, 57*(11), 1449–1477.

**62 Berg, D.H.** (1995). Laughing all the way to the bank… The power of a playful spirit at work. *Journal for Quality and Participation*, 18(4), 32–38.

**63 Costea, B., Crump, N., & Holme, J.** (2005). Dionysus at work? The ethos of play and the ethos of management. *Culture and Organization, 11*(2), 139–151.

**64 Kristiansen, P., & Rasmussen, R.** (2014). *Building a better business using the Lego Serious Play Method*. New Jersey: Wiley.

65 **Kark, R.** (2011). Games Managers Play: Play as a Form of Leadership Development. *Academy of Management Learning and Education,* 10(3), 507–527.

66 **Barnett, L.A.** (2011). How Do Playful People Play? Gendered and Racial Leisure Perspectives, Motives, and Preferences of College Students. *Leisure Sciences,* 33, 382–401.

**Barnett, L.A.** (2011-2012). Playful People: Fun is in the Mind of the Beholder. *Imagination, Cognition and Personality,* 31(3), 169–197.

**Barnett, L.A., & Magnuson, C.D.** (2013). The Playful Advantage: How Playfulness Enhances Coping with Stress *Leisure Sciences, 35,* 129–144.

67 **Baptiste, N.R.** (2009). Fun and well-being: Insights from senior managers in a local authority. *Employee Relations, 31*(6), 600–612.

68 **Chan, S.C.H.** (2010). Does workplace fun matter? Developing a useable typology of workplace fun in a qualitative study. *International Journal of Hospitality Management,* 29, 720–28.

69 **Vijay, M., & Vazirani, N.** (2011). Emerging paradigm – Fun in workplace to alleviate stress. *SIES Journal of Management,* 7(2), 24–30.

70 **Winnicott, D. W.** [1971] (2005). *Playing and Reality* (2nd ed.). USA & Canada: Routledge.

71 **Greenberg, J.R., & Mitchell, S.A.** (1983). *Object Relations in Psychoanalytic Theory.* Cambridge, Massachusetts: Harvard University Press.

72 **Abadi, S.** (2001). Explorations: Losing and Finding Oneself in the Potential Space. In M. Bertolini, A. Giannakoulas, & M. Hernandex (Eds.) in collaboration with A. Molino, *Squiggles & Spaces (Volume 1) Revisiting the Work of D.W. Winnicott* (pp.79–88). London: Whurr Publishers.

**LaMothe, R.** (2005). Creating Space: The Fourfold Dynamics of Potential Space. *Psychoanalytic Psychology*, 22 (2), 207–223.

**Schacht, L.** (2001). *Between the Capacity and the Necessity of being alone* in M. Bertolini, A. Giannakoulas, & M. Hernandex (Eds.) in collaboration with A. Molino, *Squiggles & Spaces (Volume 1) Revisiting the Work of D.W. Winnicott* (pp. 112–126). London: Whurr Publishers.

## PLAY AND EMOTIONS

**73 Dai, C.** Cameron is a graffiti artist based in Australia, and a dear friend of mine and my husband's. He has designed lots of bear graphics for me, pro bono, to support the work of Bearapy. More of his work can be found at www.daicameron.com.

**74 Li, E.** (2018, Feb 18). TEDxYouth@HongKong. *Expressing Emotions Playfully.* Retrieved from www.youtube.com/watch?v=aeOIaHbmOE0

## PLAY AND FEARS

**75 Freud, S.** [1911] (1958). *Formulations on the Two Principles of Mental Functioning. The Standard Edition of the Complete Psychological Works of Sigmund Freud XII* (pp.218-226). London: Hogarth Press.

**76 Noch Noch.** (2016, June 3). *The fearful iceberg.* Retrieved from http://nochnoch.com/2016/06/03/the-fearful-iceberg/

**Noch Noch.** (2016, May 22). *The inadequacy test.* Retrieved from http://nochnoch.com/2016/05/22/the-inadequacy-test/

**Noch Noch.** (2016, July 19). *The answer to my fears.* Retrieved from http://nochnoch.com/2016/07/19/the-answer-to-my-fears/

**77 Jung, C.G.** (1968). *Man and his Symbols.* US: Dell.

**78 Kegan, R.** (2009). *Immunity to Change: How to Overcome it and Unlock the Potential in Yourself and Your Organization.* Massachusetts: Harvard Business Review Press.

**79 Levinson, D.S.** (1986). The Seasons of a Man's Life: The Groundbreaking 10-year study that was the Basis for Passages. US: Ballantine Books.

## THE ADULT-CHILD

**80 Shaw, G. B.** (1903). *Maxims for revolutionists.* Accessed 09/07/2018 via https://archive.org/stream/ maximsforrevolut26107gut/26107.txt

## FISH FACE

**81 Li, E.** (2018) *Going MENtal: Men DO Get It.* Hosted on newsstand.joomag.com

**82 Noch Noch.** (2014, November 25). 10 years anniversary of the fish face. Retrieved from http://nochnoch. com/2014/11/25/10-years-anniversary-of-the-fish-face/

## THE WORKPLACE

**83 El-murad, J., & West, D.C.** (2004). The Definition and Measurement of Creativity: What Do We Know? Journal of *Advertising Research, June,* 188–201.

**R Roos, J., & Victor, B.** (1999). Towards a New Model of Strategy-making as Serious Play. *European Management Journal,* 17(4), 348–355.

**84 Dunne, D.D., & Dougherty, D.** (2012). Organizing for Change, Innovation, and Creativity. In M.D. Mumford (Ed.), *Handbook of Organizational Creativity* (pp. 569–583). London: Academic Press.

**85 Richards, R.** (2010). Everyday Creativity. In J.C. Kaufman, & J.R. Sternberg (Eds.), *The Cambridge Handbook of Creativity* (pp. 189–215). Cambridge: Cambridge University Press.

**86 Richards, R.** (2010). Everyday Creativity. In J.C. Kaufman, & J.R. Sternberg (Eds.), *The Cambridge Handbook of Creativity* (pp. 189–215). Cambridge: Cambridge University Press.

**87 Li, E.** (2017, November 16). Beanbags and Pingpong Tables are Useless, Inner Playfulness is Key to a Healthy Workplace. *Forbes.* Retrieved from www.forbes.com/sites/lienoch/2017/11/16/beanbags-and-pingpong-tables-are-useless-inner-playfulness-is-the-answer-to-a-healthy-workplace/

**88 Li, E.** (2015). *Desktop Playground: Transitional objects at play for everyday creativity in the workplace* (Executive Masters Thesis). INSEAD, Singapore.

**89 Aliprandi, M.T.** (2001). Antisocial Acting-out as a Substitute for the Spontaneous Gesture in Adolescence. In M. Bertolini, A. Giannakoulas, & M. Hernandex (Eds.), *Squiggles & Spaces (Volume 2)* (pp. 133–138). London: Whurr Publishers.

**Farhi, N.** (2001). Psychotherapy and the Squiggle Game: A Sophisticated Game of Hide-and-Seek. In M. Bertolini, A. Giannakoulas, & M. Hernandex (Eds.), *Squiggles & Spaces (Volume 2) Revisiting the Work of D.W. Winnicott* (pp. 65–75). London: Whurr Publishers.

**90 Statler, M., Roos, J., & Victor, B.** (2009). Ain't Misbehavin': Taking Play Seriously in Organizations. *Journal of Change Management,* 9(1), 87–107.

**91 Power, P.** (2011). Playing with Ideas: The Affective Dynamics of Creative Play. *American Journal of Play, Winter, 288–323.* Retrieved from www.journalofplay.org/

**92 Kets de Vries, M.F.R.** (2012). Get Back in the Sandbox: Teaching CEOs How to Play. Retrieved from INSEAD Faculty & Research Working Paper (2012/125/EFE).

**93 Li, E.** (2015). *Desktop Playground: Transitional Objects at Play for Everyday Creativity in the Workplace* (Executive Master's Thesis). INSEAD, Singapore.

**94 Li, E.** (2015). *Desktop Playground: Transitional Objects at Play for Everyday Creativity in the Workplace* (Executive Master's Thesis). INSEAD, Singapore.

**95 Freeman, A.M., Johnson, S. L., Staudenmaier, P.J., & Zisser, M.R.** (2015). Are Entrepreneurs "Touched with Fire"? Retrieved from www.michaelafreemanmd.com/Research_files/Are%20Entrepreneurs%20Touched%20with%20Fire%20(pre-pub%20n)%204-17-15.pdf

**96 Li, E.** (2015). *Desktop Playground: Transitional Objects at Play for Everyday Creativity in the Workplace* (Executive Master's Thesis). INSEAD, Singapore.

**97 Li, E.** (2015). *Desktop Playground: Transitional Objects at Play for Everyday Creativity in the Workplace* (Executive Master's Thesis). INSEAD, Singapore.

**HOME**

**98 Li, E.** (2015). *Desktop Playground: Transitional Objects at Play for Everyday Creativity in the Workplace* (Executive Master's Thesis). INSEAD, Singapore.

**99 Li, E.** (2015). *Desktop Playground: Transitional Objects at Play for Everyday Creativity in the Workplace* (Executive Master's Thesis). INSEAD, Singapore.

**100 Proyer, R.** (2011). Being playful and smart? The relations of adult playfulness with psychometric and self-estimated intelligence and academic performance. *Learning and Individual Differences* 21: 463–467.

**101 Book of Life.** (2018). The Golden Child Syndrome. Retrieved from www.thebookoflife.org/

**102 Book of Life.** (2018). The Golden Child Syndrome. Retrieved from www.thebookoflife.org/

**103 Noch Noch.** (2016, December 12). Letter to my daughter – and to myself. http://nochnoch.com/2016/12/12/letter-to-my-daughter-and-to-myself/

**104 Horowitz, B.** (2014). *The Hard Things about Hard Things: Building a Business When There are No Easy Answers.* US: Harper Business.

the Shaw mind
FOUNDATION

Creating hope for children,
adults and families

Sign up to our charity, The Shaw Mind Foundation
**www.shawmindfoundation.org**
and keep in touch with us; we would love to hear
from you.

*We aim to bring to an end the suffering and despair caused
by mental health issues. Our goal is to make help and support
available for every single person in society, from all walks of
life. We will never stop offering hope. These are our promises.*